Blackburn
College

Library
01254 292120

Please return this book on or before the last date below

Illus-
tration
Play 2

An Expedition to the
Extraordinary

A showcase of illustrations made from threads, paper,
crayon sticks, welded steel, unwanted garments, salvaged
woods, gun shots, imagination, meditation, cultural roots,
childhood memories and many more.

viction:ary

ad : art direction
ph : photography
cl : client
ag : agency

Content

Traditional crafts are no longer realised in its traditional ways.

Paper cut figure by Ana Ventura from Lisbon.

Ron van der Ende nailing wooden chips into place.

Preface

Thanks to the advancement of technology, traditional crafts are no longer realised in its traditional ways. Where sewing machines can be programmed to stitch, and designs can be imported to laser-cut machines and executed with the slightest mistakes, little would bother to free themselves and learn the mystique of art making passed down by time. Only until some time ago, the idea of handicrafts was brought up again with the term 'DIY' or 'do-it-yourself', first time since mid 19th century, asking people to re-taste the interesting quality of imperfection and uniqueness. Everyone got so excited — you will see girls knit on the bus and hear drillings in your neighbour's walls at times. The creative industry is no exception, as when artists started retrieving the skills and tools of handwork, craving for new ways of illustration with familiar materials and skills in the first volume of *Illustration•Play*, and later shooting physical models and products for final 2D graphical outputs gathered in *Stereographics*. The whole scene was totally energised by the mingling of human efforts and the long-been-digitalised art.

Despite the fact that some of the essential skills of delicate art have been lost forever, these products of civilisation are still affecting contemporary art in every way. From the intention to visualise thoughts and pursue beauty, to the process of making — you learn, explore and refine your skills — and the source of materials used for creation — clay, hay, wood, animal's skin or even human body, say for tattoo art — the fundamental spirit of art making today has seen no difference from the past. Perhaps only the subject and motifs, which most of the time came from livelihood, tales and myths, as well as gods and religion in days of old, or otherwise present-day crafts would be like what Kenichi Yokono (P. 200) from Tokyo suggests, 'a new approach developed by living artists after having assimilated the influence of past works', while he gave his view on the role of traditional Japanese art in new creations.

A continuation of *Illustration・Play: Craving for the Extraordinary*, the body of *Illustration・Play2: An Expedition to the Extraordinary* witnesses a significant number of unconventional approaches that have composed the new visions and illustration attitude in present scene. The word 'illustration' here is not confined to flat drawings or printings, but rather covers a range of art forms varying from embroideries and collage, to papercuttings, crafts, sculptures, bas-reliefs and installations. The media of illustration, or the way that artists 'play' with the making of illustrations, continues to be the focus of this book. Whether it is the potential of variations enabled by the properties of the material or techniques, or the natural instinct that has led artists to the particular medium or a mix of many, it is never an easy journey to get to the medium that would suit your mind and art. All in all, it requires time to gather suitable elements and new inspirations through tryouts and research.

> *The fundamental spirit of art making today has seen no difference from the past.*

Modern landscape in Gregory Euclide's eyes.

Kenichi Yokono's woodblock craft in acrylic paint.

Like Rotterdam-based Ron van der Ende (P. 210), who would spend his afternoons walking into that large second-hand store with a flashlight, rummaging in some 7000 doors and skinning them for wooden chips with their old paint layers intact. Van de Ende's bas-reliefs and collage art are based on real images, where colours and touch are given by the original shades and texture of found wood. For the past ten years, his crafts have incorporated illusions of three-dimensional objects and painterly details, such as shadows and reflections, to represent a relationship that we might seem to have neglected in real life. Parallel messages are also apparent in Gregory Euclide's (P. 160) landscape art, which rigorously recalls and deplores the 'extras' that man has added to the natural environment over time. By employing a mixture of landscape images and found materials including litter and actual artefacts taken from land, Euclide's dimensional objects raised an open-ended question, asking viewers to imagine and experience the possible changes in land through his eyes.

Equally worthy of attention is Meredith Dittmar's (P. 110) relief-like sculptures made from polymer clay. Polymer clays are thermal set plastics, which would remain soft before it is hardened by heat. It was only decades ago when art makers began to sculpt polymer clay, explaining how it took Dittmar ten years of 'hard' work before she finally feels 'uninhibited by the technical challenges of the medium' today. Dittmar's human-animals-plant-energy amalgams are all about opening up quiet spaces in viewers' souls, and through convening in that space, revealing the interconnectedness of all things. Follow this — starting from her education in computer science, then a career in interactive design, a compulsive need to create and a drive to seek — you will unravel the vital elements of Dittmar and her work.

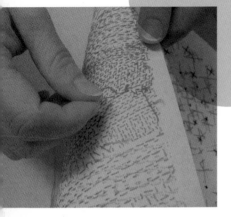

Evelin Kasikov interpreting digital print with cross stitches on paper.

The process of making has always been an expedition to possibilities.

Thousands of handcast crayons precisely arranged to form photorealistic images in Christian Faur's wooden frames.

Meredith Dittmar's sculptures and 'Guys' made from polymer clay.

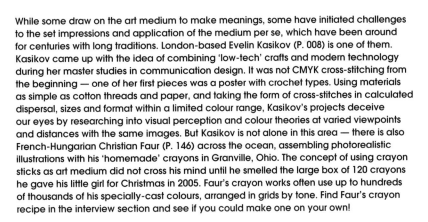

Don't sleep, wake up and see how things could be different!

While some draw on the art medium to make meanings, some have initiated challenges to the set impressions and application of the medium per se, which have been around for centuries with long traditions. London-based Evelin Kasikov (P. 008) is one of them. Kasikov came up with the idea of combining 'low-tech' crafts and modern technology during her master studies in communication design. It was not CMYK cross-stitching from the beginning — one of her first pieces was a poster with crochet types. Using materials as simple as cotton threads and paper, and taking the form of cross-stitches in calculated dispersal, sizes and format within a limited colour range, Kasikov's projects deceive our eyes by researching into visual perception and colour theories at varied viewpoints and distances with the same images. But Kasikov is not alone in this area — there is also French-Hungarian Christian Faur (P. 146) across the ocean, assembling photorealistic illustrations with his 'homemade' crayons in Granville, Ohio. The concept of using crayon sticks as art medium did not cross his mind until he smelled the large box of 120 crayons he gave his little girl for Christmas in 2005. Faur's crayon works often use up to hundreds of thousands of his specially-cast colours, arranged in grids by tone. Find Faur's crayon recipe in the interview section and see if you could make one on your own!

The process of making has always been an expedition to possibilities — you start from the basic techniques, learn from failures and push yourself to create so as to own the skills. Perhaps like what Ana Ventura (P. 076) says: Don't sleep, wake up and see how things could be different! Your perspective is one in a million! Whether you are expanding the competence of an existing technique, or experimenting with an approach that no one has taken before, there will always be something new to discover as long as you action and try. With a vibrant showcase of unparallel handworks and inspirations, *Illustration•Play2* invites you to revel in this new era of distinctiveness erected by the very playful hands of art makers from the same world we live in.

My work is printing technique in tactile form. The idea to combine craft with technology is based on my interest in the tactile, physical side of design. I have always been inspired by materials. For me, this is an important part of the design process.

The college environment at St Martins was a test ground of new ideas. I started to experiment with craft and developed CMYK cross-stitch technique during my MA course. I have no background in textiles, but this actually helped me to develop fresh approach. I worked with other craft techniques as well. One of my first pieces was a poster showing pixellated type in crochet technique.

Graphic design has a broader meaning for me now. I still work with computer besides my needles and threads.

Studio *Evelin Kasikov*

London, UK

With an MA in communication design from Central Saint Martins College of Art and Design, Evelin Kasikov specialises in editorial design and illustration. Her work is about craft within the context of graphic design and explores how we see and experience printed matter. She will be exhibiting new works with jewellery designer, An Alleweireldt, in May at a show themed 'Craft meets Music' at Craft Central, London, and a group show 'Ornamental', also in London.
Portrait by Sarah Roesink.

Printed Matter / Image
cl: Central Saint Martins College of
Art and Design (MA degree project)

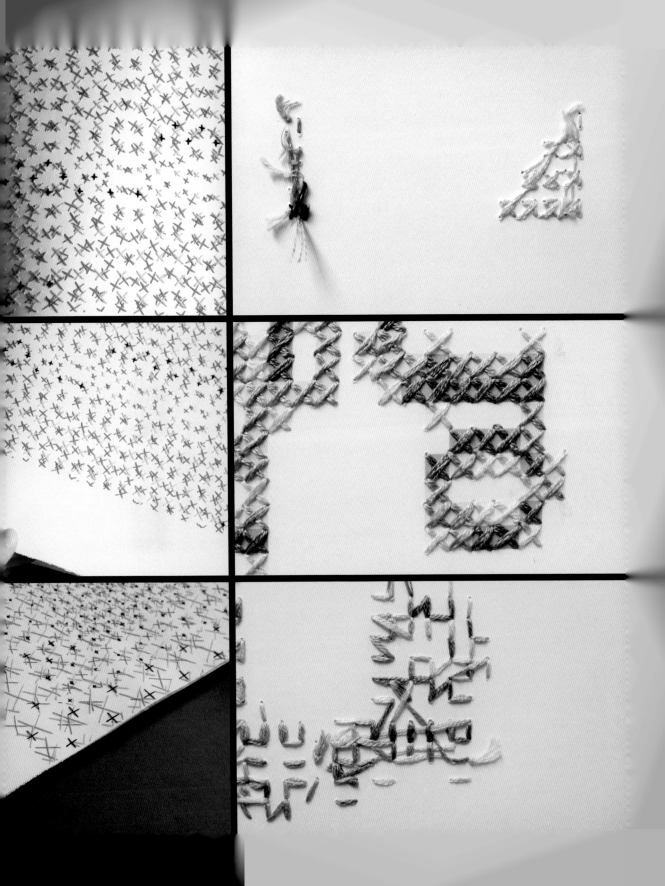

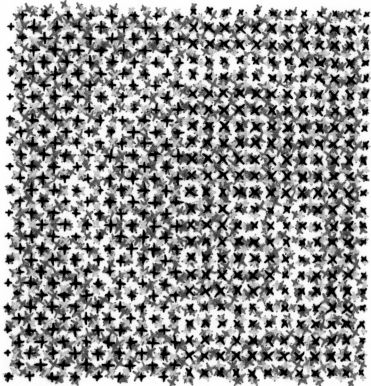

Handmade CMYK
cl: Central Saint Martins College of
Art and Design (MA degree project)

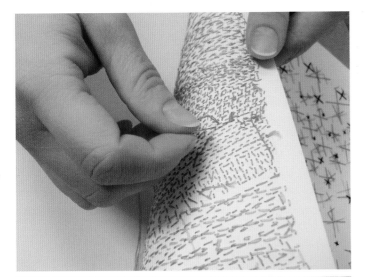

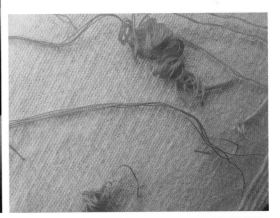

Printed Matter / Type
cl: Central Saint Martins College of
Art and Design (MA degree project)

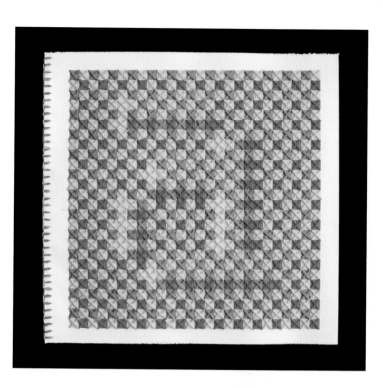

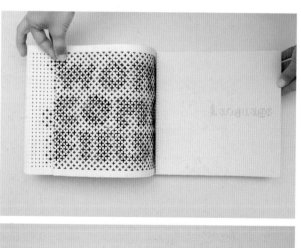

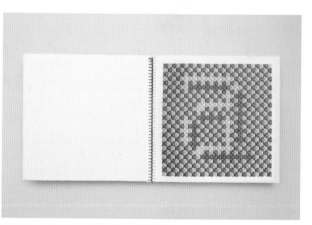

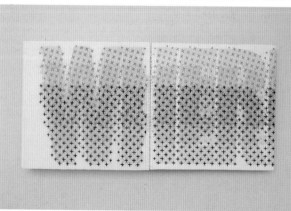

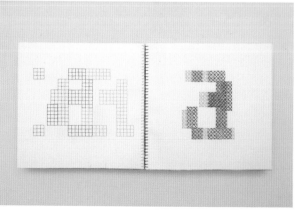

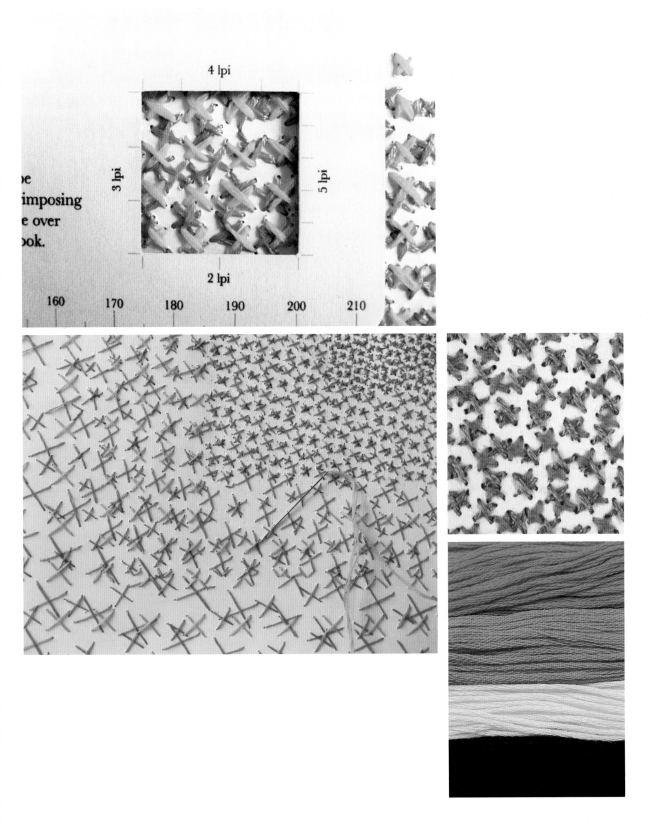

Type and Cities
cl: Neue Magazine

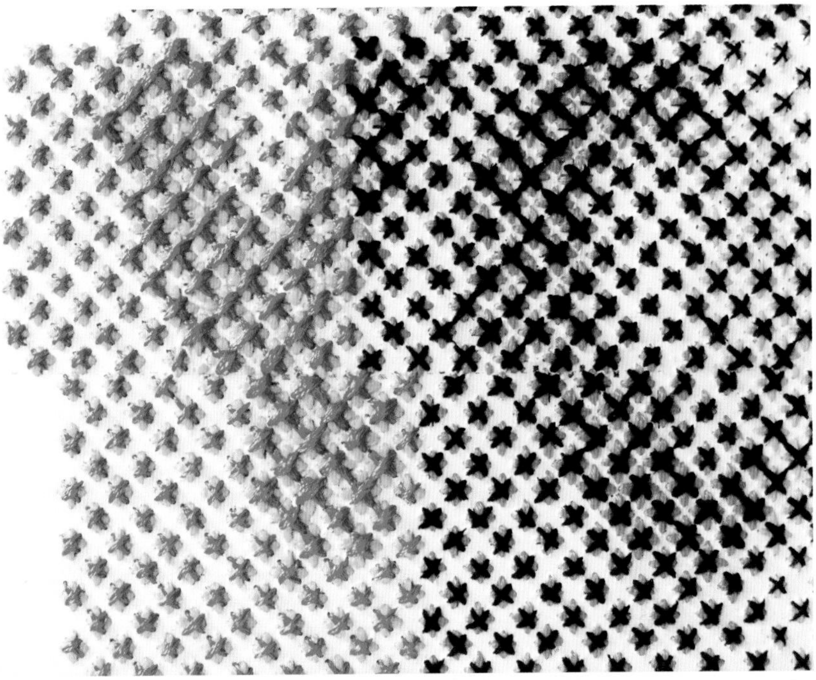

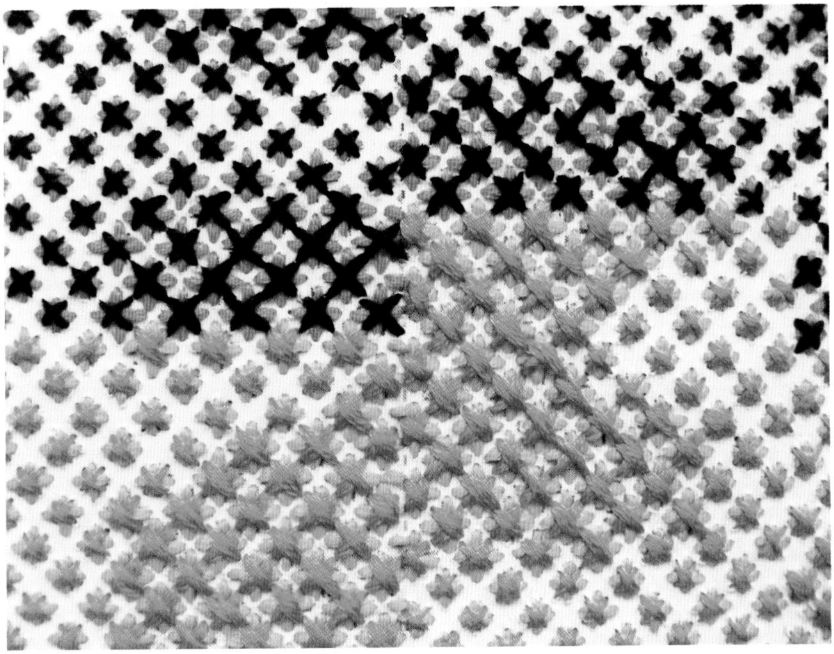

One reason for me getting into paper craft was my love for paper. Prior to quilling, I mainly focused on hand-drawn illustrations.

My name *Yulia* was the starting point of my experiments on 'paper-graphics'. I was looking for an eye-catching typographic image of my name for my self-promotional brochure, but my hand-drawn variants were not satisfactory. Then I remembered the quilling technique that I once used quite a long time ago. My brochure was never published, as I had really got into paper work.

Through my projects, I'm trying to take quilling to a new level of conveying meaning in the context of graphic communication and fine art. I take my work to explore the potentials of the technique as a serious form of self-expression.

Yulia *Brodskaya*

Herts, UK

Born in Moscow, Yulia Brodskaya has a love for many creative practices, ranging from origami and collage, to textile painting and the more traditional fine art practices. Following her move to the UK in 2004 and her master studies in Graphic Communication in University of Hertfordshire, she continues to explore ways of innovative paper illustrations, by bringing together the things she likes most – typography and paper.

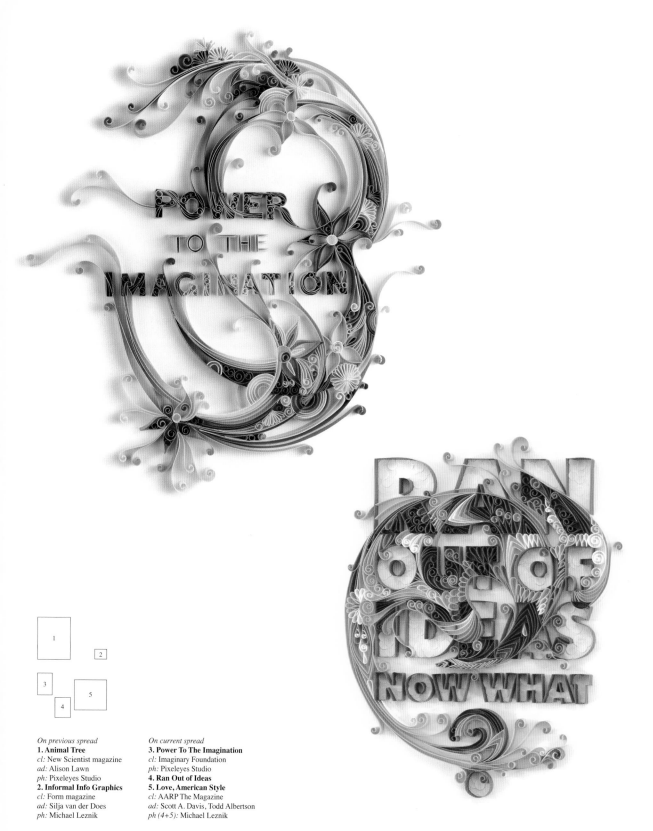

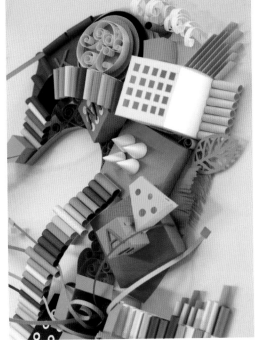

Cadbury Project
cl: Cadbury (Ireland)
ad: Keith Doyle
ag: Publicis QMP
ph: John Ross

MADE with a GLASS and a HALF FULL of REAL IRISH MILK

I'm really interested in the alchemical nature of paper cutting – the way that an everyday material that we all use, consume and dispose of all the time can be transformed into something precious, beautiful and meaningful.

I was always interested in dioramas as a child and my paper cutting first came about when I was trying to make surrealist dioramas in university. I turned to paper art because the medium is flexible and ephemeral – it is relatively easy to manipulate and cut as you want. The level of detail that can be achieved in cutting paper is amazing.

I was also fascinated by the shadow play that is achieved with layers of paper. I'm always finding something interesting about it, there's always a new avenue to explore.

Emma *van Leest*

Melbourne, Australia

Born and raised in Melbourne, Emma van Leest graduated from RMIT University in 2000 with a bachelor's degree in painting. She continues to live and make art in Melbourne but travels frequently to Asia. The Australian artist draws inspiration from a variety of sources including fairy tales, Asian art and religious relics, as well as artists, such as Johannes Vermeer and Joseph Cornell.
All photos by John Buckley Gallery.

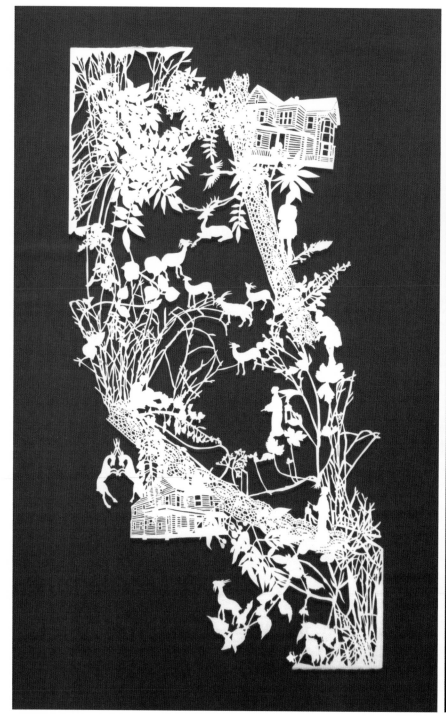

The Dowsed Heart

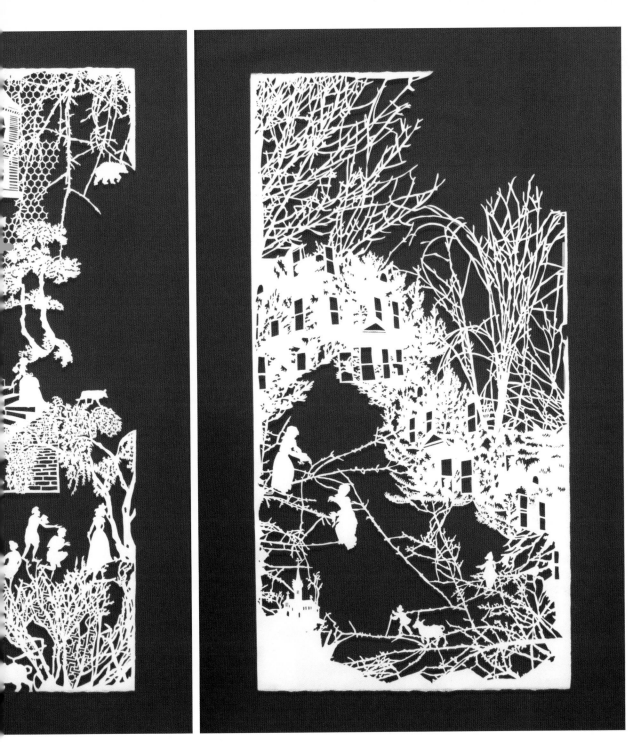

My work is often about the elusiveness of what could be called magic – the unseen yet existing force that people have forgotten about, the greater universe and relationships. Then comes the characters who pursue it, where bravery and battles are involved.

The human ability to imagine things and the resilience to conquer fears and downfalls have a great impact on me, while curiosity is probably the trait that moves my art forward. Researches on mythologies, galaxies, artists, etc. helps create a catalog of information that inspires visual stories.

I think loneliness is not such a bad thing. It forces you to meet yourself and perhaps find things to make better. Looking at the stars in a night sky makes me feel a range of things, from fear and terrible loneliness to utter admiration (not so different from looking at someone you love).

Dan-ah *Kim*
New York, USA

Korean-born Dan-ah Kim has moved to Mexico and later attended Pratt Institute in New York, where she now divides her time between making art and freelancing in film and television. Kim is drawn to the chaotic and collaborative film environment as well as the isolated experience of making illustrations, as it grants her a chance to work on her own narratives. Kim works primarily in gouache, ink and threads.
Portrait by Aileen Son

1. Seek Me Out Courageously
2. Findings Of A Voyager

Dan-ah *Kim*

My work expresses the idea of a story, fable or tale, and attempts to sort out the past and create new beginnings. How these stories have affected my culture is represented through a combination of book and animal sculptures, drawings and writings.

For the past several years I have been working with books as a sculptural material. Paper is a thin form associated with delicacy. I am finding ways to present its depth. Since the encounter with text has now become mostly an onscreen experience, I am tunneling into vintage hardbound texts to explore the uncertain future of the book itself. I often add fine-line drawings or found images, in addition to cuttings, to re-script the story.

Book and stories are pulp surrogates for my life. In my work, I express a worry about the line between remembering and distorting the story.

Jennifer *Khoshbin*

San Antonio, USA

Raised in an art family comprised of master carpenters, ceramic artist, filmmaker and new media artist, Jennifer Khoshbin was exposed to art at an early age. Born in Philadelphia and now a mom to two, with a professor husband, Khoshbin is currently planning on starting her MFA in 2011 and restoring a small 1915 home to start her own contemporary gallery.

1. Rank
2. Make That You See
3. You're A Liar And Cheat

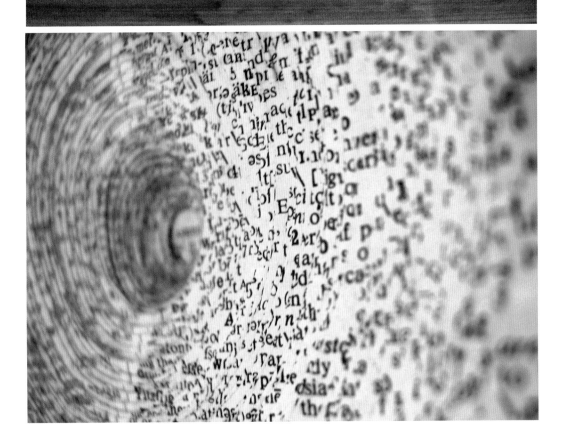

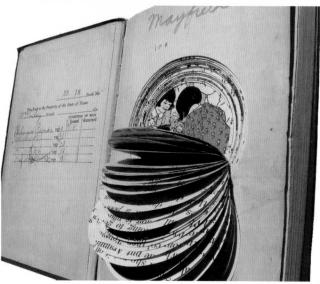

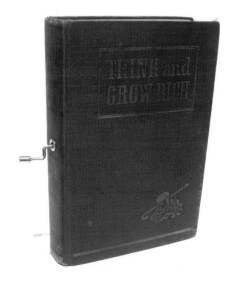

1. There's A Kitten In Here
2. Think And Grow Rich Music Book
3. Swinging My Way Back
ph: Toni Frissell

I am always endlessly fascinated by the character and stories behind the things that have been owned and used. By appropriating parts of their stories and re-imagining my own tales, I give these things a second life with my imagination going berserk.

As a person who sews, I have a special liking for texture and small details. I like the contrast between silk and felt, and the way that pinking shears turn the edges of fabric into tiny waves. Being a photographer by education has conversely given me an appreciation of the future, the color of light and turned me into an archivist for my family's old photographs.

I fell in love with my flatbed scanner and the unique way it captures details and lets me play with scale, e.g. the sense of depth in *Nest*. My work currently reflects the bundle of pretty contradictions where my interests in the past and the future meet.

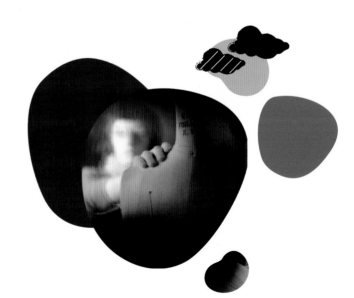

Sarah *Trahan*
Berkley (Michigan), USA

Sarah Trahan is an artist and educator. Holding a BFA in photography from the College for Creative Studies, Detroit, and a MFA from Cranbrook Academy of Art in Bloomfield Hills, Michigan, she currently teaches an array of undergraduate photography classes involving both traditional and alternative image-making techniques.

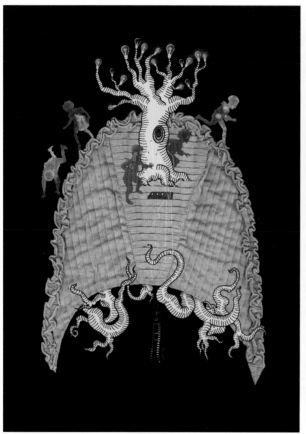

1. Cheesecake
2. Best Wishes
3. Portrait 1

1. Portrait 2
2. Limbs

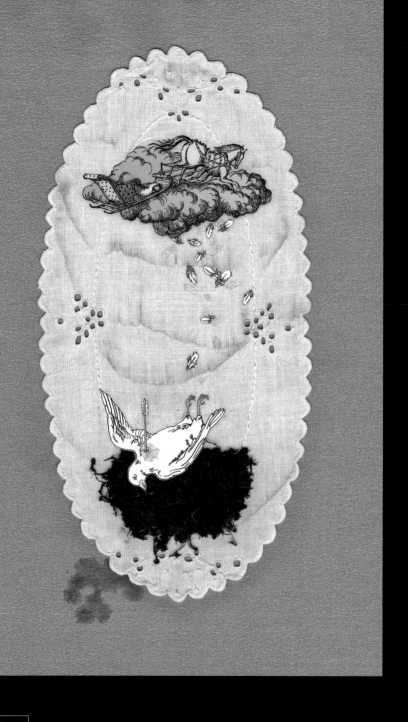

I like creating a world where everything is soft and bright, and there is always some good to be found. It's not that I'm pretending that there's nothing bad in the world, but when there's sadness or pain, I would try to show it in a way that the viewer feels hope.

Computers really help to retain delicate pencil lines on top of fabric surfaces. The first work I made with computer was *Lighthouse*. I always made illustrations with collage and paint in school, where they could be displayed the way I made them. And it became more natural to use computer techniques while I work as an illustrator now, as they eventually end up being printed flat in magazines.

I am very thankful to be an illustrator at this point in time as people now are very open to non-traditional techniques in illustration. I will never get tired of making images because there will always be something new to discover.

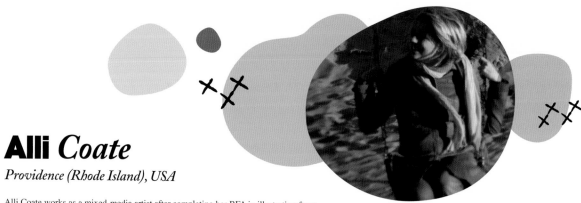

Alli *Coate*

Providence (Rhode Island), USA

Alli Coate works as a mixed-media artist after completing her BFA in illustration from Rhode Island School of Design in 2008. She has always been fascinated by handicrafts and she loves working with scraps of paper, fabric, thread and finding extraordinary things in the everyday.

Alli *Coate*

1. Lighthouse
cl: So Rhode Island Magazine
2. **Providence Patchwork**
3. **Swimming Pool**
cl: Providence Monthly

1. Take The Scenic Route
2. Multiplication

Love & Loss

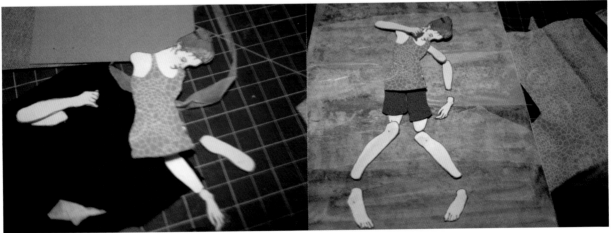

ANA VENTURA ©

I like to create figure illustrations and use them in several materials like paper, fabrics and tape. It's more like playing with images and giving other sense to them. That's something I love to do.

I started creating paper cut illustrations in 2006 when Sharilyn Wright at lovelydesign invited me to participate in her 'beautiful scrap of paper project'. She was sending out paper bits from her former projects to artists from around the world to make things they like. I now gather paper leftovers myself and, when I find good combinations of paper, I make a new doll. Always a different and unique one.

I'm always seeing faces and figures everywhere, and, as a creative person, I like to play with that. It's like a message: don't sleep, wake up and see how things could be different! Your perspective is one in a million!

Ana *Ventura*

Lisbon, Portugal

Born in 1972, Ana Ventura trained herself to paint with an engraving major in the University of Lisbon. Before she graduated in 2000, she made an internship in the École nationale supérieure des arts visuels de La Cambre, Brussels, under the Erasmus Programme in 1999. Ventura is currently a freelance illustrator, who has been working regularly with Galeria do Centro Português de Serigrafia since 2006.

On previous & current spread
CUT+PASTE
in collaboration with
Centro Português de Serigrafia

ANA VENTURA ©

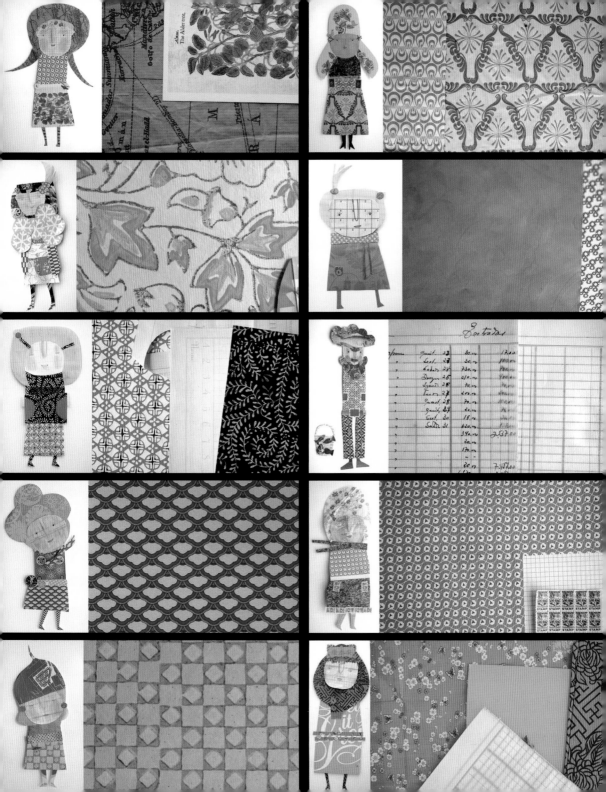

On previous spread
1. Paper Dolls

On current spread
2. Harum Scarum

Reality has a multiple structure. I feel like everything has four layers of meanings – a main layer that varies with time or by individual, with other layers existing at the same time. Sometimes I imagine a structure model for things and our mind. The idea came from a sacred tree I saw in Iwate Prefecture in Japan. To me, the tree has four layers – the sky, the tree, the rocks and water. The lower layers represent primitive, raw natures and uncontrollable things, while the higher it goes, it becomes more intelligent, conscious and socialised.

Though there might be natural influences from traditional Japanese art in my work, my works are much more personal. Traditional art was developed from time-honoured custom with strict basic forms, but my life style is far from those.

Mayuko *Fujino*
Tokyo, Japan

Mayuko Fujino is a self-taught papercutting artist who began her practice in 1999. It was Japanese traditional stencil dyeing that led her to her unique paper art. Fujino is currently based in Tokyo while planning on a year-long stay in New York after her next show at Megumi Ogita Gallery, Tokyo, in July.

On previous spread
E(cstasy) Cut
1. Body

On current spread
2. Melt
3. Still
4. Underwater

Umi No Hi (The Day of the Sea)
5. Sail

1. Red Wave
2. Heavenly Bodies
3. Shigan Higan

Arikui Abduction
1. Landing
2. Dai-ba

3. Heavenly Bodies

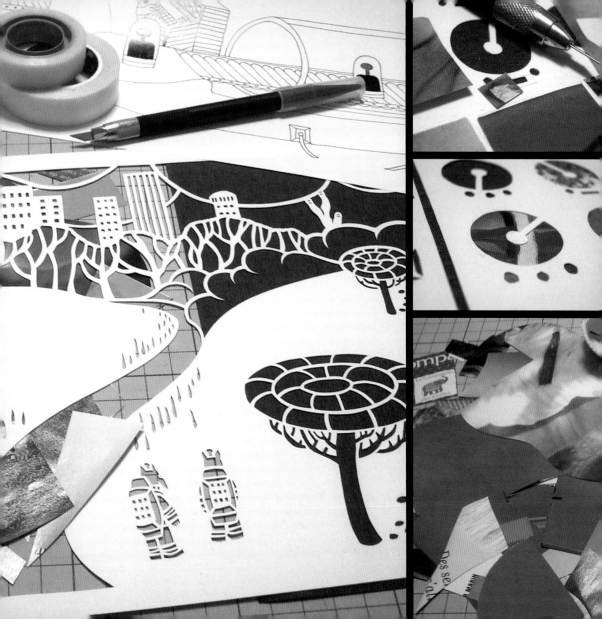

Paper to me is a living, breathing thing. It has a life of its own. I just try to redirect that energy into something that feels animated and alive. When I talk about experimenting with different types of paper, it would mean the exploration of shapes, bends and round edges. I want to manipulate paper in the least invasive way, to keep the integrity and feel of it.

Being able to think out of the box is most important to my work. It's what keeps the journey interesting and challenging. And, going outside the box means leaving your comfort zone, taking risks and giving it that little extra effort.

Hopefully, from my work, you'll remember there is always a positive future, and you'll smile despite all the bad things we hear from the news. I always remind myself to keep forging ahead. I never think I can't learn more from life.

Jeff *Nishinaka*

Los Angeles, USA

The beginning of Jeff Nishinaka's career as a paper sculptor was quite unintentional. He has always wanted to be a painter, but his school assignments on the experimentation of different media for drawing has brought him new thoughts. Nishinaka is a Los Angeles native, and an art graduate from the Art Center College of Design, Pasadena, California.
All photos by Ed Ikuta

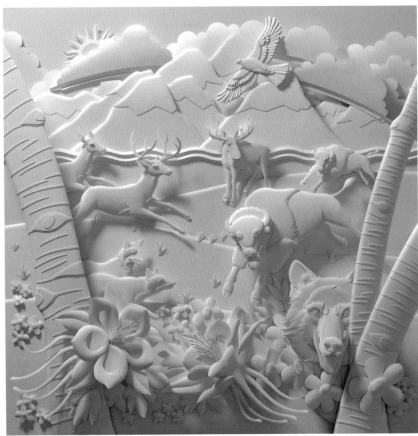

<table>
</table>

	1	
2		3

On previous spread
1. Tiger Mask

On current spread
2. Brooklyn Bridge
cl: Private commission
3. Preserve
cl: Sprint Press

1. **Dragon**
cl: Peninsula Shanghai Hotel
2. **El Sereno Phoenix**
cl: Barrio Action Youth & Family Center
3. **Dragon & Phoenix**
cl: The JC Group
4. **Imperial Dragon**
cl: Paper Cut

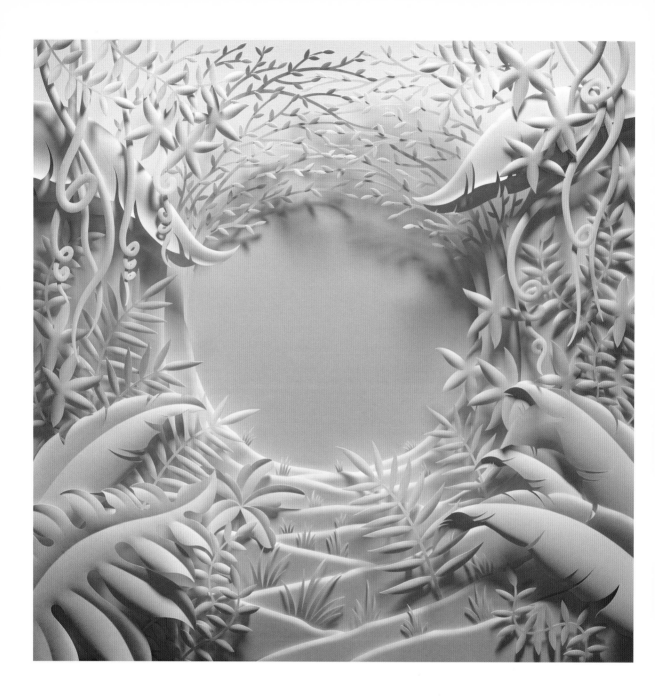

1. Secret Garden
cl: O.A.R./Atlantic Records
ad: Mindy Ryu
2. University of Colorado Hospital Campus
cl: University of Colorado Hospital

3. USA Philatelic
cl: U.S. Postal Service
4. United States of Avex
cl: Avex (Japan)

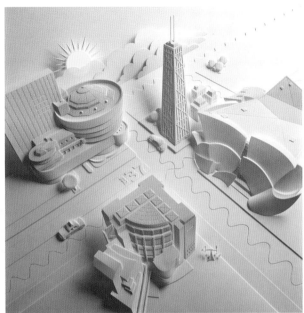

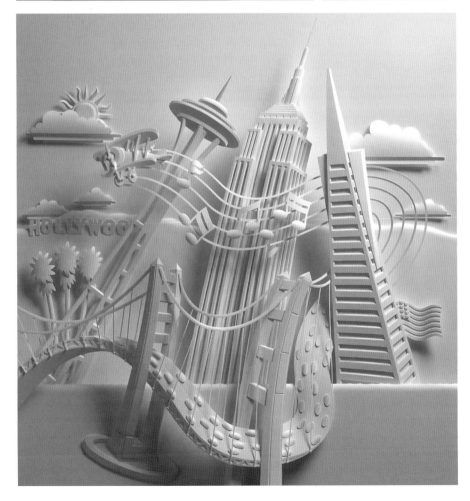

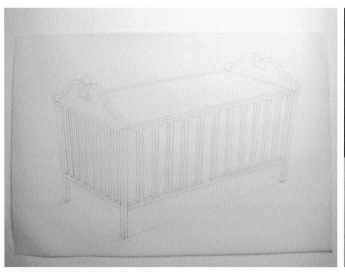
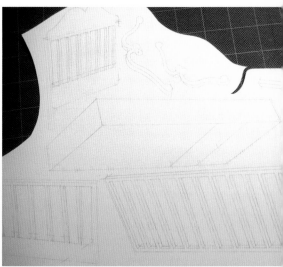
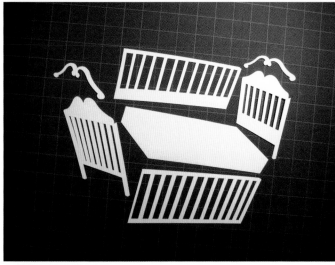

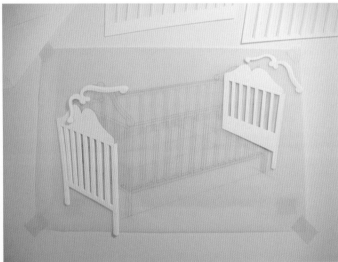

After working with polymer clay now for over ten years, I am finally at a point where I feel uninhibited by the technical challenges of the medium, as it demands constant innovation to create desired effects.

Before I begin work on a set of pieces, I gather and fill my brain with diagrams, images and words on topics that are of current interest to me (or the client). I listen to lots of talks on spirituality, philosophy and the sciences. I let all this settle, then try to create from an open quiet space and see what comes out.

My work is all about this open space.

Meredith *Dittmar*

Portland (Oregon), USA

Meredith Dittmar is an artist living and playing in Portland, Oregon. Born near Boston Mass, she grew up in a world of pet pigs, horses, hay-forts and spy games. Dittmar's human-animal-plant-energy amalgams contain threads of common elements and colours to express deep levels of union across themes of biology, technology and consciousness. She sees the act of spontaneous artistic creation as part of a larger practice of being present, and a way to better understand herself and reality.

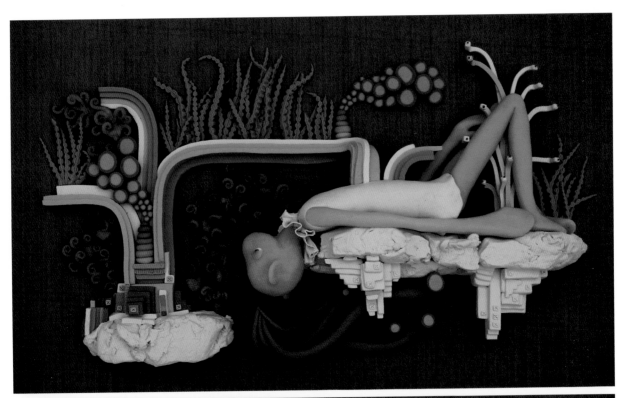

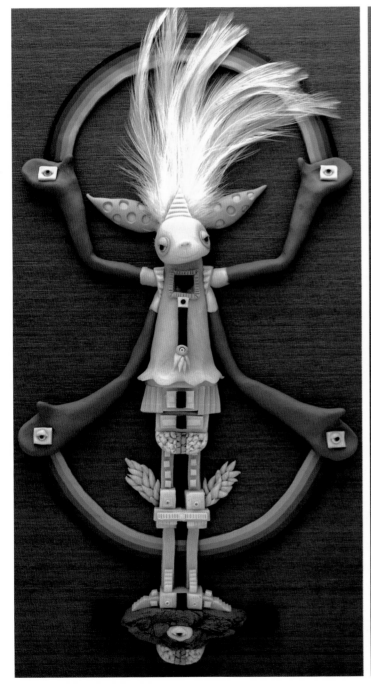

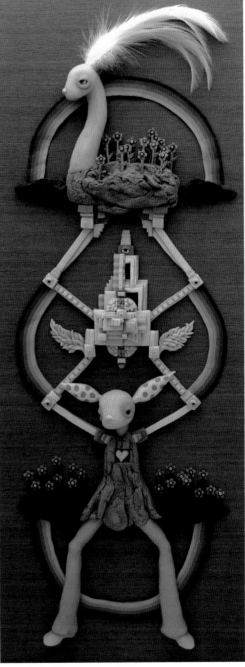

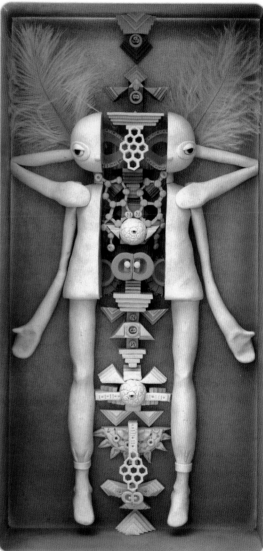

Lab
1. Socket Seat
2. Inner Makeup
3. Big Self
4. Distorted Self Reflection
5. Space Within A Space

Milk
1. A Trinity Of One
2. The Infinite Pool
3. Expansion
4. The Silence Presides
5. Matter Of Heavens And Earth
6. Hold The State
7. Grasping The Source
8. Complexity Of Mind

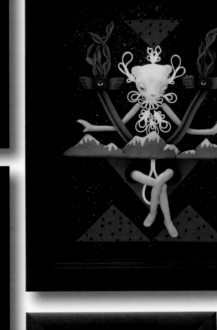
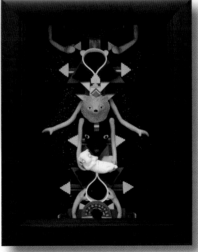

Hotcakes
1. White Collar #1
2. Lichen
3. Indocentric
4. Guts

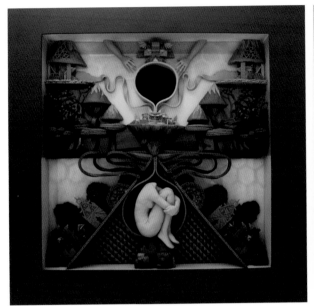

Levine
1. A Momentary Summit
2. Face The Phenomena
3. Inter-thinking

I remember someone described my work as 'a dynamic mix of craftsmanship and contemporary visuals that lead into a somewhat neo-absurdist work that lives a life of its own', which is spot-on.

I like it when the viewer finds quick access to the art. A joke, haptically appealing material, simple forms and supposedly cute characters - to me all that are friendly, uncomplicated invitations to contemplate a piece. Then, through closer inspection, the viewer might discover what stands beneath the friendly surface - social research and criticism, psychodrama, tragedy and joy of life. I believe in evolution and the winding path of life.

Nina *Braun*

Berlin, Germany

Nina Braun was a visual arts student in Hamburg, Germany before dropping out for her own skateboarding business, *Sumo*, in 1998. With a love for mixing supposedly 'outmoded' handcraft techniques with contemporary matters, Braun turned to art after six years of urban design for the brand. She now takes the liberty to explore different materials and processes by means of sculptures, installations, textile pictures and paintings, objects and cartoons.
Portrait by Felix Gebhard

On previous spread
1. Gang
ph: Heliumcowboy Artspace

On current spread
2. Circle Of Friends
ph: Felix Gebhard
3. Big In Japan
ph: Heliumcowboy Artspace

Nina *Braun*

1	
2	3

1. Expansion
2. Diffusion
3. # 003 - 102 (Geisterrave)
ph: Heliumcowboy Artspace

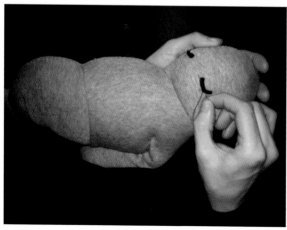

1. In The Countryside
**2. Take Your Time But
Don't Take Mine**
3. # 002
ph (all): Felix Gebhard

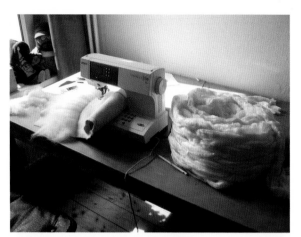

Tumulus
ph: Felix Gebhard

My creations do not always tell stories. Sometimes I do them by simple aesthetic pleasure. But the story begins when a human figure shows up in my work.

This is not life that is ironic but my way of looking at it. When I re-present people in my collages and paintings, I never do it with malice but rather with sympathy. Sometimes I add to my illustrations a bit of irony to mock my characters in a friendly way, as in *Superman du terroir* and *Golden Boys*. I make fun of their proud postures.

My philology studies taught me to read between the lines and puzzle out what the narrator suggests in the text, while my journalism studies trained me to transmit information as accurately as possible. Certainly these studies have influenced my way of illustrating: I suggest and I transmit.

Anastassia *Elias aka*
Chadou Yuma

Paris, France

Born in Russia in 1976, Anastassia Elias aka Chadou Yama moved and settled in France in 2001, where she first launched out into children's illustration full-time. She started showing her painting works in Paris since 2003. 'Chadou Yama' is a phonetic pun invented by Anastassia's husband, Jean Elias. They have published their first book, *Grand-mère arrose la lune*, together in 2006.

On previous spread
**1. Roi des Papillons
(King of the Butterflies)**

On current spread
**2. Superman du Terroir
(Rustic Superman)**

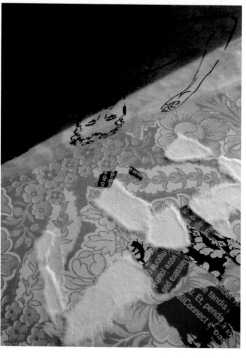

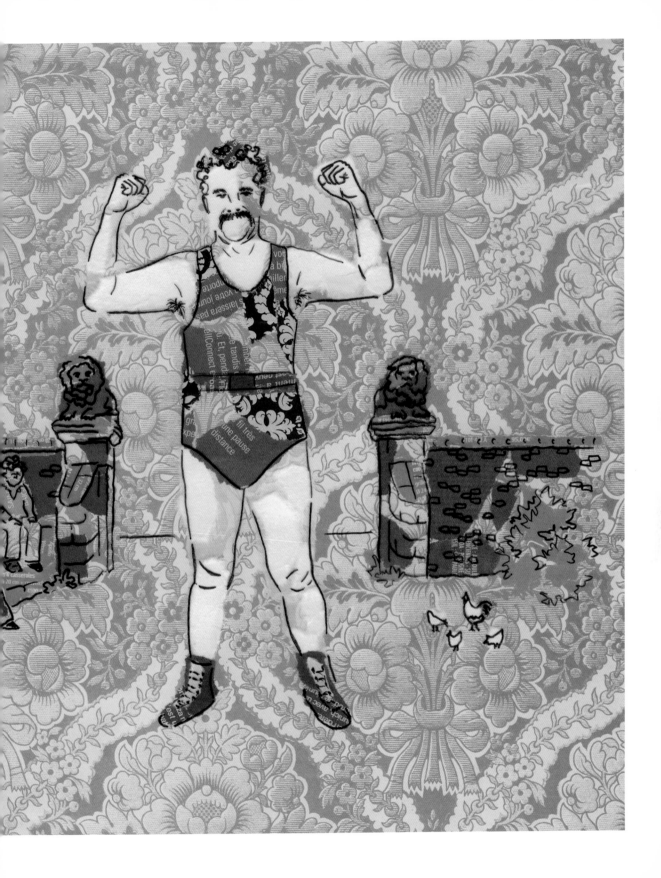

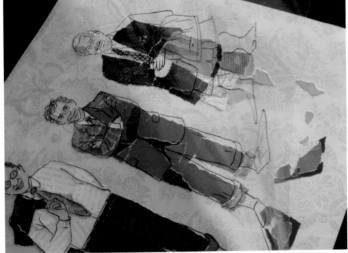

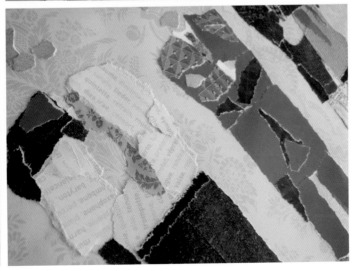

Golden Boys

1. Balcon (Balcony)
2. Passants (Passers)

1. Mauvais Temps (Bad Weather)
2. Métro (Metro)

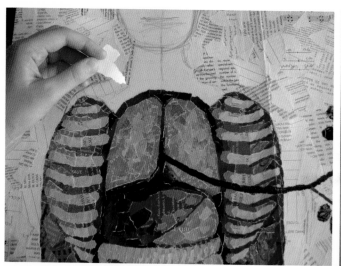

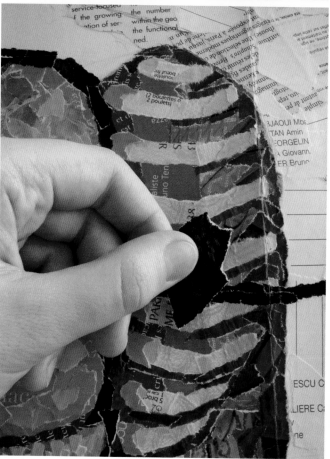

À Cœur Ouvert (Open Heart)
ph: Jean Elias

In my work, I often try to develop systems to express my thoughts and ideas, so that the medium and the message appear as one. I think of it like a game, with a set of axioms established at the outset through the limitations of the material or forms from which the work is constructed. This then dictates what can and cannot be 'said' within the boundaries of the chosen medium. This material limitation can also be a strength, as there is the potential to contain thoughts and ideas in unique ways, so that the 'medium' can become the 'message'. This intertwining of form and function can be seen in my most recent work of crayons and shredded paper.

Christian *Faur*

Granville, USA

With a bachelor's degree in physics and a MFA, Christian Faur is Director of Collaborative Technologies at Denison University, Granville, Ohio, where he teaches courses in digital media and animation among other things. Faur's work encompasses areas of painting, sculpture and new media. His recent pieces include a paper sculpture made from shredded versions of the United States Constitution, protesting against the abuses in Guantanamo Bay.

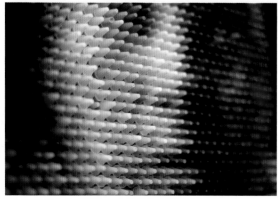

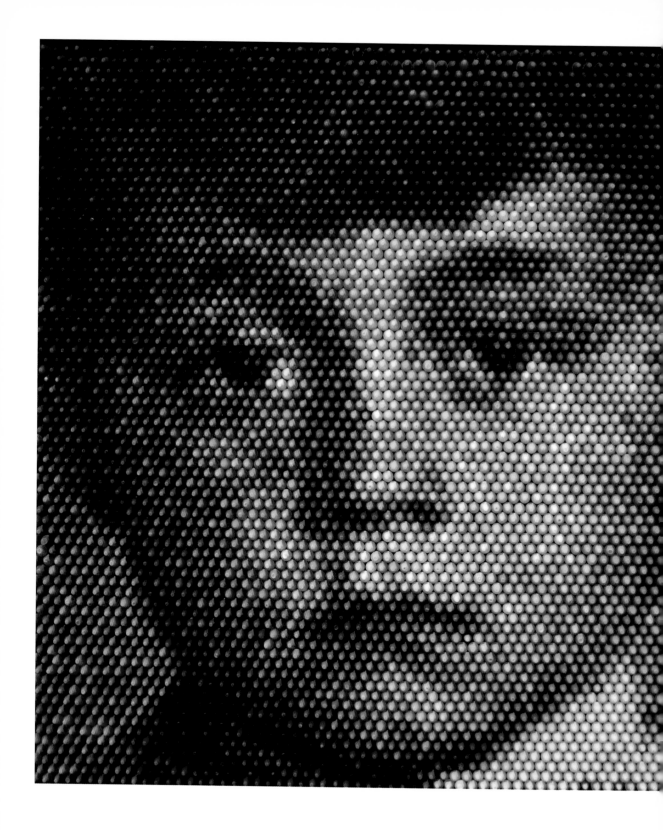

1. Blue Boy
2. True Color Series Child 1

1. Depression Era Boy
2. Depression Era Girl

Christian *Faur*

1. Depression Era Man 1
2. Depression Era Man 2

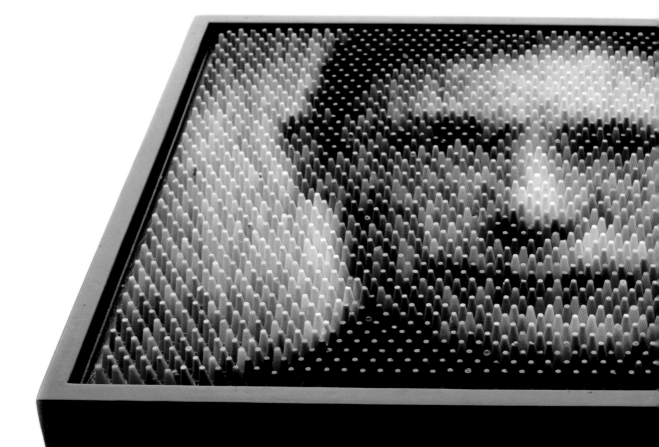

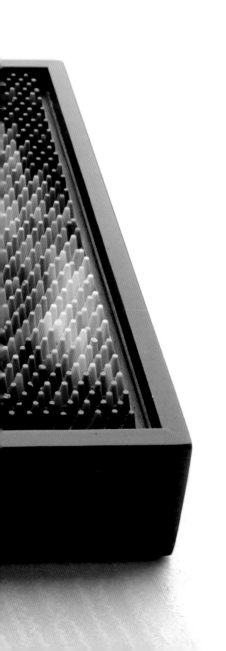

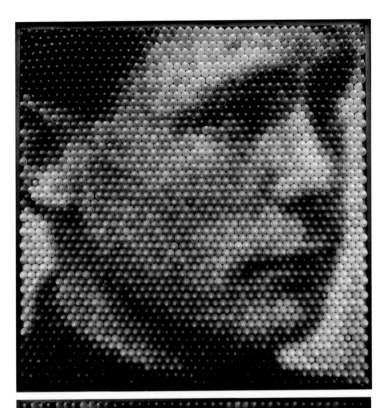

<table>
<tr><td>1</td><td>2</td></tr>
</table>

1. Euler
2. Untitled 6500

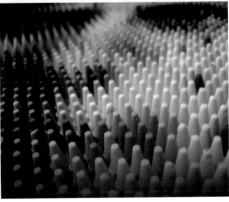

My work explores the relationship between the projection of idealized landscapes, my own experiences in the land and the creation of landscape art. My recent compositions carry a blend of imagery composed of scenic landscapes drawn from memory, photo transfers and actual artifacts from the land such as pine needles and found plastic.

There is a correlation between the way we create 'landscape' and the way we interact with nature. In all our efforts, from the gardens of Versailles to the faux countryside of Capability Brown, our intentions have been to prove our mastery, understanding and dominance over nature. In my work the faults of this way of thinking become apparent and the 'nature' we have made today is presented to the viewer.

Gregory *Euclide*

Le Sueur, USA

Gregory Euclide is an artist and teacher living in the twin cities of Minnesota. His attraction to the landscape can be traced back to his childhood when he was allowed to roam around the rural landscapes of Wisconsin. Euclide has developed an appreciation for contemplative experiences within the natural landscape since. The complexity and interconnectedness of the environment has cast a profound impact on him, forming the content and conceptual framework for his future work.

1. Concerning What Fiction Dissolves
In Your Top Branches
2. Following Became My Pooled
Stretch Of Karst
3. I Was Only The Land Because
I Liked The Predictable Stillness
4. Held On History's Material Desire
5. Scoring A Chorus In The Crests
That Could Not Be Owned

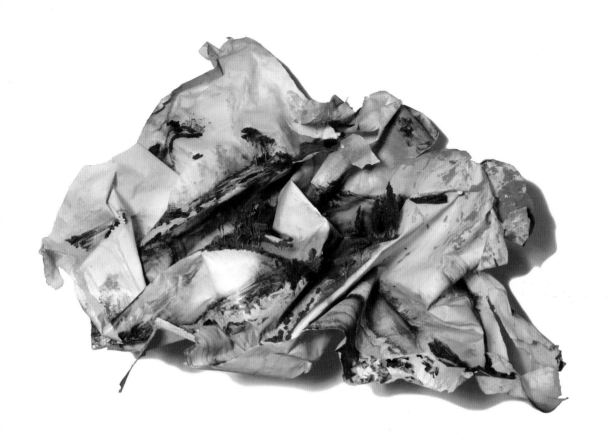

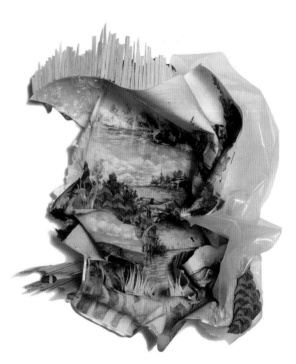

1. Capture #1
2. Capture #9
3. Looming
4. **Struggling Swept Canyons Focus Toward Tangents**

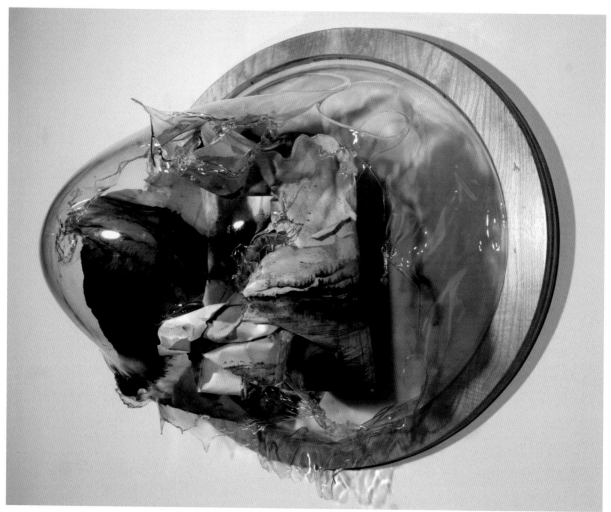

1. A New Kind of Quiet,
Warm In The Air, Bursting
Forth From The Furrow
2. I Was 30 Feet In The Air
When The Gray Floated
Down All Around Me

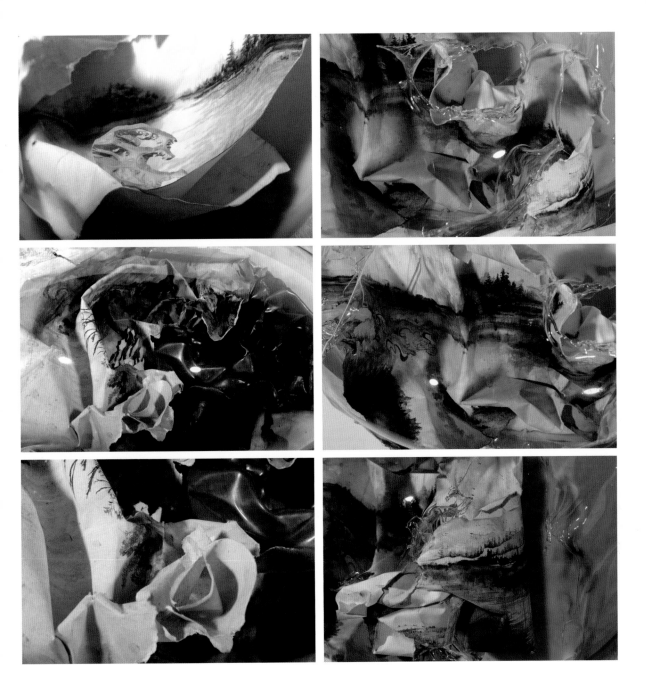

Banal understanding of beauty and utilitarian things always interest me and inspire my creations, which explains the use of fragments of pop culture, the so-called 'kitsch', in my art. They are like 'quotations' in the new context – they will lose their clearly negative content and become my personal experience and point of view.

Ordinary humans and mundane fragments of his or her life acquire exceptionally important meanings in my works, while recognised icons of beauty are less important to me.

Banal and simple, these roses, peonies, violas and marguerites are flowers from a Lithuanian girl's garden. I often use them as a simple language, e.g. flowers for 'beauty', rust as the metaphor of antiquity and lids and buckets for the domestic and material side of life.

Severija *Inčirauskaitė-Kriaunevičienė*

Vilnius, Lithuania

With a master's degree and bachelor's degree in textile art from the Vilnius Academy of Fine Arts, Lithuanian artist Severija Inčirauskaitė-Kriaunevičienė raises doubt in the traditional hierarchy of art and takes pleasure in things that are only insignificant details in most people's eyes. In her art composed of drilling and cross-stitching, you will find the colours of Lithuania by the metals and rusts.

On previous spread
1. Once Upon A Time In The Soup

On current spread
2. Morning Trio

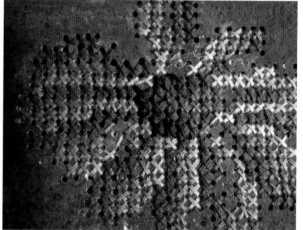

1. Direction
2. Autumn Collection

1. Between City And Village
2. Object For Comparison

Way Of Roses

16

My work is about physical and social observations. I think of things in terms of compositions - whether that be an object, a line of text or a social situation.

To me, it's important for a work of art to be open and accessible. I look equally for harmony and discordance and find them similarly revealing and fascinating. I've been imbued with a sense of social awareness and hence choose to deal with these issues as I sometimes see them in my work. Finding and examining the subtle manners of communication of and between humans for me is all about exposing the balance and symmetry or lack thereof in our everyday existence.

Frank *Plant*

Barcelona, Spain

American-born Frank Plant studied sculpture at the University of the Arts in Philadelphia, Pennsylvania. After finishing his BA in fine arts in 1993, he moved to Amsterdam and developed his drawings in steel, and later to Barcelona and began to diversify the materials he uses. Welded steel has always been the principal medium in Plant's work, alongside photography, painted wooden backgrounds, light boxes, motors, sensors, sound and music.
Portrait by Richard Salas

On previous spread
**1. One Day You Too Can
Work In Advertising**

On current spread
2. WH(Y)?

17

1. **We're All So Complicated**
2. **Liberty**
technical support: Remi Melander
3. **Marcel & Sara**
cloth doll: Melkorka Reynisdottir

26

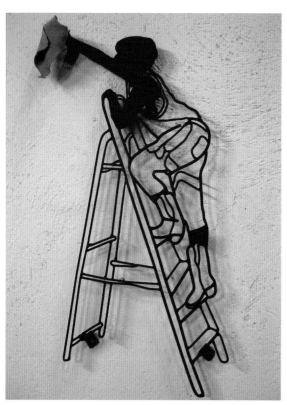

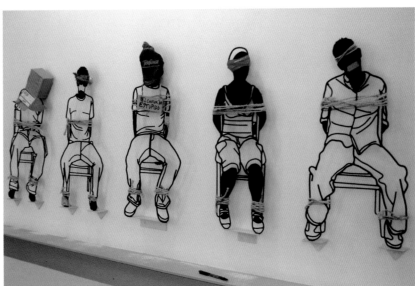

1		4
	3	
2		5

1. Anna Going For The Hard To Get Spots
2. Anna Hace Lo Suyo
3. The Stupid Consumer
4. Hostages
5. We Know What You Are Thinking

1
2
3
4

1. **Fun On The Playground**
2. **The After From the Before**
cloth doll: Melkorka Reynisdottir
3. **Rita**
4. **Stay On Message**
ph: Richard Salas

You'll see persons and objects, mostly very colorful and in oddly situations. Maybe you didn't see this combination of things before, but in a jiffy you'll realize that these things naturally belong together. For some reasons, these pictures have a calming effect. They don't tell lies. They are my contribution in a competition of truth. My favorite truth.

I grew up with the Eastern Bloc. Life was hard, and the prevalent color was grey, the real color of communism. I was sure you'll need something nice in a world with little delights of 'sensory perception', just like the many cute and folksy fixtures in the Polish houses (as in my parents' house even today).

Old cartoons seemed fusty dusty nowadays but I love them anyhow. For some reasons it feels like home. I suppose my first influences were "Nu, pogodi!" and "Lolek and Bolek".

Roman *Klonek*

Düsseldorf, Germany

Polish-born artist Roman Klonek discovered his passion for woodcut printing when he studied graphic arts in Düsseldorf, Germany, in the 1990s. The many whimsical creatures in Klonek's woodcut posters often display strong influences from East European cartoons. The special feelings he has for foreign places and cultures are evident in the presence of characters, such as Hanji from Japanese and Cyrillic.

1 | 3
2 |

1. Mitkommen
2. Kuma
3. New In Town

1. Follow Us
2. Over
3. Without Saying A Word
4. Around The World

Doggone

I always try to express my ever-changing feelings and my judgment in my work, so as to capture the beautiful moments of this dark and ominous world we live in. Although many of my work evoke motifs of fear, the more powerful sense of 'pure innocence' would appear to break these images, just like my attitude towards my art.

Colour variation is inevitably limited in my art. The red and white were initially adopted to associate with the image of a Japanese wooden seal when I first saw a woodblock, but then, I realised red would actually evoke the thought of blood and leave a strong impression to my audiences.

Recently, I start using black since I began sketching with a Suiboku-ga brush. I want to bring this technique or expression to my work.

Kenichi *Yokono*

Tokyo, Japan

Born in Kanazawa in 1972, Kenichi Yokono trained himself to practise traditional Japanese woodblock carving at Kanazawa College of Art in Japan. Yokono has been showcasing his highly detailed carved woodblocks, rather than the prints, in cities like Tokyo, Amsterdam and New York. As an artist, he believes that it is his mission to expand the audience's imagination with inspirational work.

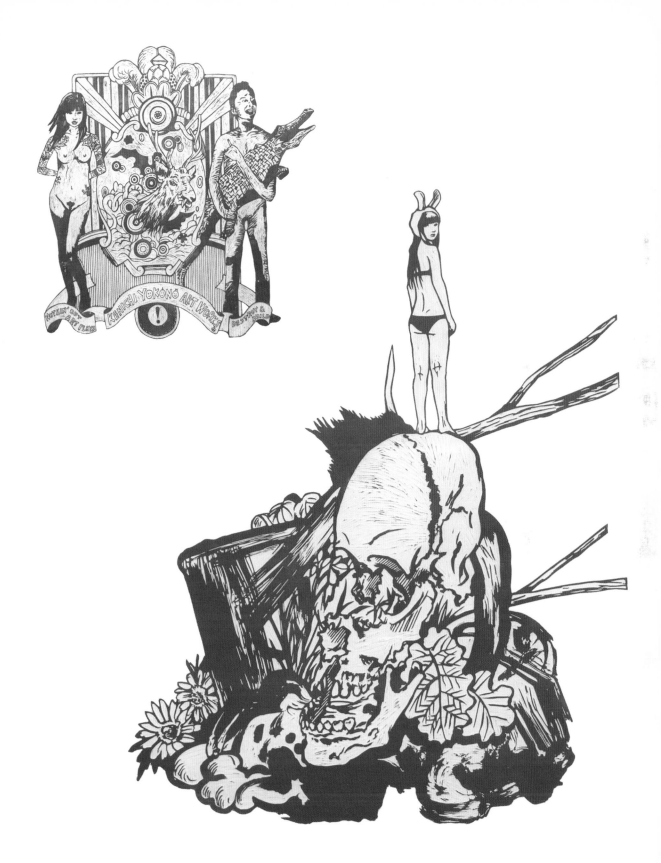

On previous spread
1. emblem2
2. skull and girl

On current spread
3. flower
4. chandelier 3
5. skateboards girl 5 dive

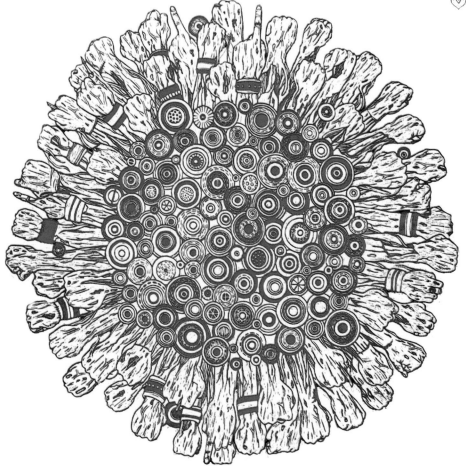

1. girl and bear
2. the scene
3. bury deep

BEAR
HEAD

スマイル

1. vomit
2. addict
3. phantom of cubicle

The significance of my boyish perspective is my quest to better understand our relationship to the objects we surround ourselves with. I like to re-present things we have forgotten about and bring them back to life by executing them in a forceful and involving way.

The one time I failed to transform a vision into a physical piece was when I tried to incorporate two humans into a work. The figures just looked like cartoon characters at the scale I attempted. The piece lingered in my studio for three years until I decided to finish the remainder of the piece without them. The piece turned out great in the end.

For the past ten years my work has taken me further down a path that has led me to a place where anything is possible. I can't wait to see where I will go from here!

Ron *van der Ende*

Rotterdam, the Netherlands

With both parents working in the same construction company, Ron van der Ende was no stranger to the look and smells of woods before kindergarten age. He has experimented with a host of different materials, including sound and movements, in his sculptures after studying sculpture at Willem de Kooning Academy, Rotterdam and before settling for used wood. He specialises in wall-mounted bas-reliefs from salvaged wood.
Portrait and photos by Vincent Mentzel

On previous spread
1. Stadbus (Town Bus)

On current spread
2. Schooner
3. Vissersboot
(Fishing Trawler)

1. Peekskill
2. Sea Ice Runway
Fire-Engine (Foremost)
3. DS I (Snoek)
4. DS II (Pallas)
5. Silver Machine
(Lotus Turbo Esprit 1983)

Axonometric Array
cl: WORM

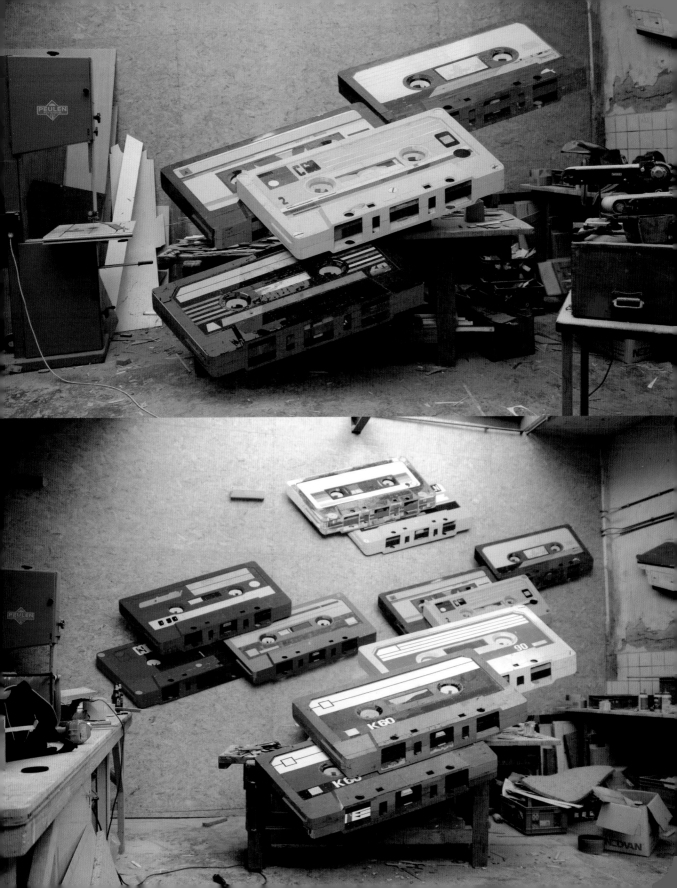

1. Space-Ops (Mc-Murdo)
2. Engine House 5750/Loods 5750
3. Flagmans House/Baanwachtershuis

1. Vostok
2. Ørnen (De Adelaar/The Eagle)
3. Endeavor (Apollo15)
4. KEF Speakers
5. Akai-VT100 (Open Reel
Portable Video Recorder)

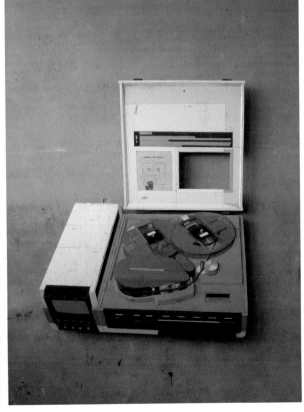

The terms 'gun' and 'weapon' are practically interchangeable. From hunting to war, self-defense to target practice, the gun has been a symbol of power and destruction. Art and entertainment often take the same approach to guns – with some using high-speed film to capture a bullet slicing through its target, and others melting guns into sculptures.

Aiming to make guns the focus instead of an accent in my work, I set myself a goal to take away the destructive powers from them. Things really clicked when I took a canvas and a gun into the woods and started experimenting by shooting a single-file line right into the canvas in 2004. It was at that point that I realized I would be using my gun solely as a tool to create my work.

Walton *Creel*
Birmingham, USA

Brought up in a rural part of the States and familiar with firearms from a young age, Walton Creel is a self-taught artist who uses his .22 caliber rifle and fires bullets into reinforced and painted aluminum to make art. After years of working with video and installation art, Creel decided to incorporate guns as a tool into his work and set his goal as to 'deweaponize' guns. *Deweaponizing the Guns* is an ongoing series presented in instalments, with 'wildlife' the subject for his first series.

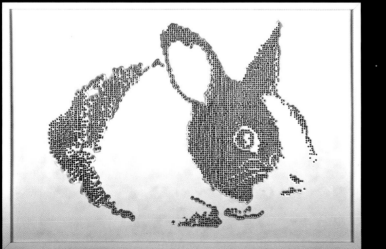

1. Owl
2. Opossum
3. Wren
4. Squirrel

Based on a combination of traditional disciplines and experimentation with dimensions and the use of unconventional materials, our products are inspireted by an essential familiarity with the ready-made and the archeological qualities that found objects possess. The energy that reveals underlying meanings and depicts the significance of mass-produced refuse on our society is often encapsulated in the results.

Through a common aesthetic, we create work with a universal message. Taking recycled objects as their medium and the guidance of the unrelenting amount of information that fuels today's mass consciousness and its subversive parallels, we explore ways to reinvent historic themes and classic icons while still commenting on contemporary culture.

Guerra *de la Paz*

Miami, USA

Guerra de la Paz is Cuban-born duo, Alain Guerra and Neraldo de la Paz, who has been consistently producing collaboratively since 1996. Composed mainly of discarded clothing, their work surrounds sculpture, installation and photography, referencing the politics of modern conflict and consumerism alongside symbols of faith.
Portrait by Douglas Voisin

Florida

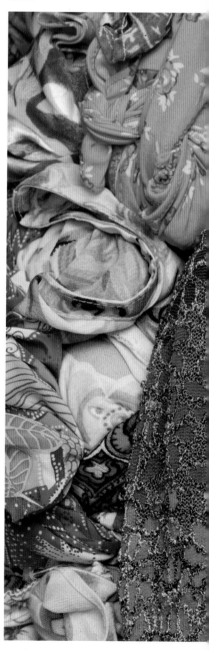

1. Four Seasons
2. Eden
3. Oasis
4. Spring-Sprang-Sprung

My cut paper works were developed primarily through my drawing practice. As an avid keeper of sketchbooks, for years, I have explored the co-mingling of abstract figuration and transcendental themes in my daily drawing practice.

Many of my current works are related to an ongoing series, which I think of as my 'inner beasts'. They are inspired in part by characters in mythology world, as well as personal deities, representing various states of mind while I am in the studio. I also see them as a reaction against the current economic environment – in times of crisis, people turn to religion and faith. I get the same sense of solace in the studio.

I am interested in a kind of aesthetics of plentitude, and I want my work to express a sense of abundance and exuberance. I get a lot of inspiration from visual density, which keeps me positive and energized.

Michael *Velliquette*

Madison, USA

Currently a faculty associate in the Art Department at the University of Wisconsin–Madison, 38-year-old Michael Velliquette is the recipient of six artist residencies at organisations, including ArtPace, San Antonio; SÍM, Reykjavík; and the Kohler Co. Arts Industry Program. His work is included in the Progressive Art Collection, Cleveland, and Western Bridge, Seattle.

On previous spread
1. Lil' Pinky
Courtesy of DCKT Contemporary

On current spread
2. Humbaba
3. Clown Beast
4. Together We Forget,
Alone We Remember
5. Happy Minotaur

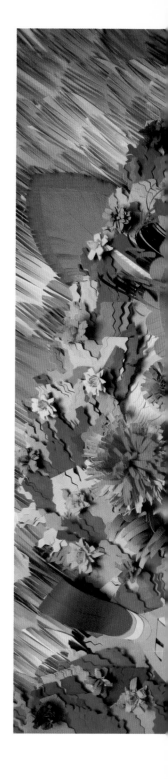

1. Snuggie
2. Mishaabooz
Courtesy of DCKT Contemporary

1. Serpent (Ruby)
2. Serpent (Lapis)

My art is about many things, but most often I reference people or stories that I find interesting and I feel the need to tell in one way or another.

Jesus Malverde, for example, is one of those characters. Malverde stole from the rich to give to the poor, and has unofficially become the patron saint of drug lords. He is not condoned by the church and yet he has a massive following. The irony this character brings, and the extent of drug culture penetration into everyday life, including the church, is what I find especially interesting.

My family is from Sinaloa, Mexico, where drug trafficking has become the mainstream and a huge part of the contemporary culture. These stories are still part of my family history today.

Ana *Serrano*

Los Angeles, USA

Ana Serrano is the first generation Mexican American born in Los Angeles, 1983. Inspired by both cultural contexts in her life, her work bears reference to those in low socio-economic positions, with particular interests in their architecture, fashion and informal economies, as well as their customs and beliefs. She has recently graduated from Art Center College of Design with honours.
All photos by Julie Klima

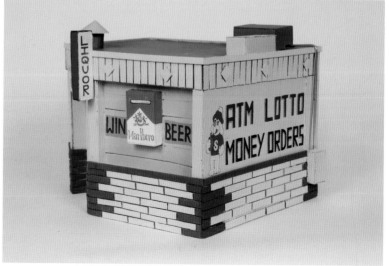

On previous spread
1. La Dolce Vita

On current spread
2. Movieapolis
3. La Liquor
4. Lety's

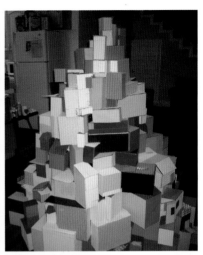

Interview

A casual conversation with the 24 artists who have managed to find their treasures of life, from the very same world we live in.

Alli *Coate*

1. How would you describe yourself?

I'm just a girl who makes things... I try to do the best I can at whatever I'm doing, and find the beauty in every part of life. I try to be optimistic but sometimes I'm very sad — that's why I like to make happy art.

2. What is your origin? What does your origin mean to you?

My heritage is mostly English and German, but I don't think about that much. I try to think more about the similarities between all people and how we can learn through our differences.

3. How do you describe what you're doing?

To me, this is art a person can live with. It is not meant for fancy galleries — there is nothing wrong with that, but I've always liked to make practical things.

4. What do you find most playful and exciting in the creative process?

I love combining different techniques that I've never used together. Growing up, I was constantly drawing and I loved embroidery and crafts; it was so exciting when I brought them together!

5. Where do you get your inspirations? How do they inspire your creation?

All the things I love find their way into my creation. I love birds and trees! I read a lot of blogs, too, and am always inspired with new ideas and images.

6. What's in your toolbox? Can you introduce us the tools and materials you use?

I use 2B pencils, my computer, lots of tracing paper (I like to draw my finals over loose sketches), a simple sewing machine, fabric, and thread.

7. Who in the field catches your attention most recently?

There are really too many illustrators I love to name them all, but lately I really like Camilla Engman, Katie Daisy, Shanna Murray, Gemma Correll, and Shannon Rankin.

8. Do you keep a collection of something as a hobby (not for work!)? What's the charm about?

I collect fabric! Lots of vintage fabrics. I love the patterns, the colors, the feels, and that the pieces have history. This didn't used to be for work, but now it has found its way in.

9. Your art proves that computer techniques could actually enhance handicrafts without taking away the quality of imperfection. Do you see a future in this direction?

I see a trend of this — using computer techniques without erasing all the hand-made charm — and I certainly think it will continue! It bothers me when computer images are too polished.

10. Please close your eyes and draft the first image in your mind.

Ana *Serrano*

1. How would you describe yourself?

a daydreamer, image hoarder, sculptor, film enthusiast

2. What is your origin? What does your origin mean to you?

i was born in los angeles, my family is mexican. to me, being mexican american is a unique experience that i love being a part of.

3. How do you describe what you're doing?

working as an artist.

4. What do you find most playful and exciting in the creative process?

the very beginning! when the idea pops in your head, and you can't think of anything else!

5. Where do you get your inspirations? How do they inspire your creation?

they come from everywhere, places, customs, myths, kitsch, pop culture, folklore, lifestyles, . . .

6. What's in your toolbox? Can you introduce us the tools and materials you use?

lots of cardboard, hot glue gun, scissors, x-acto knives, colorful paper & bright paints.

7. Who in the field catches your attention most recently?

nick cave & olaf breuning

8. Do you keep a collection of something as a hobby (not for work!)? What's the charm about?

teacups & folk art from different countries i've visited.

9. What kind of message you would like to bring out in your sculptures? What do you have to say about drug trafficking and the life of ethnic minority in your community?

the sculptures on drug trafficking are a commentary on society's glorification of that lifestyle & a look into the customs & myths of those individuals.

10. Please close your eyes and draft the first image in your mind.

mittens! my hands are freezing :-

Ana *Ventura*

1. How would you describe yourself?

A lucky girl, full of energy in a permanent creative brainstorm.

2. What is your origin? What does your origin mean to you?

I'm Portuguese. I think the best thing about be Portuguese is the climate and the food.

3. How do you describe what you're doing?

illustrations, Graphic design, photograf, art!

4. What do you find most playful and exciting in the creative process?

ALL the process until find the final Product.
The most playful is to reach a good materialization of the idea.

5. Where do you get your inspirations? How do they inspire your creation?

Everything around me is an inspiration. I'm always looking around with an artistic perspective, taking pictures and framing details with my eyes.

6. What's in your toolbox? Can you introduce us the tools and materials you use?

Lots and lots of papers full of drafts, pencils, pens, my photo camera and my computer (MAC) with internet connection.

7. Who in the field catches your attention most recently?

Always the internet and the big range of creative people that have design and illustrations blogs and sites that inspire everyone.

8. Do you keep a collection of something as a hobby (not for work!)? What's the charm about?

Little and vintage toys like miniatures, some natural treasures that I like to pick when I travel and special I have big box full of my "pocket memories" - tickets.

9. How would you describe the relationship between your family, yourself and your art?

To work and create I need time to be alone and to be with my family I need time too. I try to balance both sides but it's really hard because the creative process doesn't appear at the regular family time.

10. Please close your eyes and draft the first image in your mind.

Anastassia *Elias aka Chadou Yama*

1. How would you describe yourself?

By the words: curiosity, patience, humor

2. What is your origin? What does your origin mean to you?

I was born in Russia. The only sense that my origin has, that it gave me a culture. It is added to the culture that I acquire myself.

3. How do you describe what you're doing?

I think my works tell stories. I try to show the beauty of simple things and the everyday life. However it is not sentimental, sometimes it's ironic.

4. What do you find most playful and exciting in the creative process?

Trying to translate an idea into an image. Looking for solutions when it is difficult. Testing or inventing new techniques.

5. Where do you get your inspirations? How do they inspire your creation?

I am inspired by people around me, the anonymous. Ignore all of them allows me to invent the stories. Other artists inspire me too. They push me to expand my explorations.

6. What's in your toolbox? Can you introduce us the tools and materials you use?

For collages I use scissors a cutter a few tens of kilograms of paper. For painting I use brushes and paint. Recuperated materials expect their use: plastic caps, burnt-out bulbs.

7. Who in the field catches your attention most recently?

Mia Liu, Isabelle Tournoud, Heinz Stangl, Ahmad Nadalian, Willy Verginer, Sonia King, Hadieh Shafie...

8. Do you keep a collection of something as a hobby (not for work!)? What's the charm about?

I cut out of the TV program the sheets dedicated to the movies I enjoy. I paste them in a notebook, currently the third. Each movie title reminds me of a story — it's better than a photo album.

9. There's quite a range of paintings and crafts in your portfolio – on a myriad of themes and in distinct styles – bravo! Honestly, how did you split up yourself?

It allows me not to be bored, not to have a sense of repetition. Since I am interested in many things, splitting myself is not an effort, it's natural.

10. Please close your eyes and draft the first image in your mind.

Christian *Faur*

1 How would you describe yourself?

I like to think of myself as thoughtful and generous in how I interact with people around me I am not a terribly social person, but I do like exchanging ideas with smart and creative people.

2 What is your origin?   What does your origin mean to you?

My mother is an immigrant from Hungary and my father was from Southern France I was born in New York City, in Hell's Kitchen. That name stayed with me. French was my first and only language until I irrecoverably lost it.
We never rested. Life was a continuous stream of packing and unpacking. Very unsettled and often unsettling. People came and left. We never had enough money for anything but it made me into who I am now and that's fine with me. I have a lot of material to digest and as an artist I am continuously inspired by the vicissitudes of my life I am grateful for that.

3 How do you describe what you're doing? I make art.

4 What do you find most playful and exciting in the creative process?

For me, the 'creative process' always means creatively expressing myself in my art, which is visual art. It provides me with a language that no other creative or intellectual medium can. If I were a writer that process would have a different character.

5 Where do you get your inspirations How do they inspire your creation?

From the world we live in and how smart and intelligent people make sense of it. Often from poetry, but even more so from physics, from math, and sometimes from music. Clever and elegant expressions of ideas and thoughts, whether they come from the sciences or the arts, inspire me because they make me want to enter the human dialogue.

6 What's in your toolbox? Can you introduce us the tools and materials you use?

I am a packrat of ALL materials I can use for creating objects and have experimented and worked with almost everything out there. I like discovering the potentials these materials have, which has allowed me to develop and refine various techniques. I make pretty much everything that I need myself from raw materials. That allows for a lot of freedom from the limitations of store-bought, manufactured artist's materials. I also make the tools I need to work with these materials. I have a lot of equipment, saws, heat lamps and what used to be the darkroom, is now the computer for me, so with new technologies there are further potentials.

For the crayon work specifically, I make the crayons from scratch with bees wax, damar varnish, and high quality pigments. The intensity of the colors I can achieve is amazing. Encaustic holds the color beautifully. I make molds to produce the crayons and literally make them by the thousands.

7 Who in the field catches your attention most recently?

The artists: Anselm Kiefer , Gerhard Richter, Oscar Munoz's, Tom Freedman, Tara Donovan, Do Ho Suh.

8 Do you keep a collection of something as a hobby (not for work!) What's the charm about?

I don't separate art from my 'other' work, or art from my 'other' life - for me it's all one.
And, as I said, I collect everything I can use.

9 Sometimes you cast your own crayons' for accurate colours that are not manufactured for sale.
 How many special tones have you bred?
 How many crayon sticks do you have in stock?

Every crayon work is made up of it's own specially casted color.
For the newer TrueColor Series, each panel has over
180 different individual colors arranged in a grid by tone.

10. Please close your eyes and draft the first image in your mind.

Dan-ah *Kim*

---

1. How would you describe yourself?

Introverted ninja...

2. What is your origin? What does your origin mean to you?

Born in Korea and raised mostly in America, moving often.
It's made me restless.

3. How do you describe what you're doing?

Telling stories with pictures.

4. What do you find most playful and exciting in the creative process?

Making mistakes, getting angry, then finding ways to
make them work for me.

5. Where do you get your inspirations? How do they inspire your creation?

History, films, travel, cities, the natural worlds... This is the
short list. Things I find interesting I want to share with others by
incorporating them into my
work.

6. What's in your toolbox? Can you introduce us the tools and materials you use?

Paints, brushes, micron pens, archival glue, needles, thread,
blades. And I love paper for their colors and texture.

7. Who in the field catches your attention most recently?

Recently I've fallen for Tomokazu Matsuyama's work!

8. Do you keep a collection of something as a hobby (not for work!)? What's the charm about?

Books! Reading was my first love. And pictures of my cat, who
is sometimes mean to me but I am still weirdly mad about him.

**9. Did you ever try to illustrate scenes for your own movies? How is the experience of making
art and movies different from each other?** I've contributed lots of art to films I've
worked on, as well as draw things I'd like to turn into my own films
someday. Working on films can be crazy! Lots of people, things to keep
track of, last minute problem solving. Making art is obviously more personal.

10. Please close your eyes and draft the first image in your mind.

← Gusgus with crazy eyes.
(Right before a good pounce)

Emma *van Leest*

1. How would you describe yourself?

A professional artist. Any thing after that gets confusing.

2. What is your origin? What does your origin mean to you? I am Australian with a Dutch father. My origins mean I have a lot of freedom and opportunities as well as an interest in seeing the world - Australians love to travel.

3. How do you describe what you're doing?

I would say I make very detailed paper cuttings of imagined fairytale worlds. It's something I get asked a lot."

4. What do you find most playful and exciting in the creative process?

The most exciting aspect of the creative process is the unexpected discovery, when your work takes a turn even you would not have predicted.

5. Where do you get your inspirations? How do they inspire your creation?

I get a lot of inspiration while travelling, from reading, from my childhood. All these sources become part of the miniature worlds I create.

6. What's in your toolbox? Can you introduce us the tools and materials you use?

Most important - my stencil knife and blades! Also a cutting mat, glue, masking tape, foam core, rulers. And of course, lots of different paper!

7. Who in the field catches your attention most recently?

Michael Veliquette - his papercuts are sculptural, bold and vital. He is so highly skilled and pushes the medium.

8. Do you keep a collection of something as a hobby (not for work!)? What's the charm about?

I have a collection of shadow puppets - I try to buy a puppet whenever I travel. The Indonesian wayang kulit ones are most beautiful.

9. You have been travelling around to countries like Indonesia and China to study their traditional art and art-making techniques. Tell us what you see! Anything NOT to be missed?

Every country has something amazing to reveal - I could fill a book with all the things I've seen. Meeting other artists and craftspersons is the most exciting thing you can do.

10. Please close your eyes and draft the first image in your mind.

It's Delhi - I'm going back for a visit in a few weeks and I'm very excited!

Frank *Plant*

1. How would you describe yourself? curious, inefficient, I procrastinate a bit disorganized

2. What is your origin? What does your origin mean to you? I'm from the U.S. and it being a young culture I feel it's quite dynamic and vital. I feel these are two things I get from my culture

3. How do you describe what you're doing? As a drawing in steel...

4. What do you find most playful and exciting in the creative process? There is a moment, a space rather when I am creating that opens up all my ideas for future pieces. Very exciting!!!

5. Where do you get your inspirations? How do they inspire your creation? See above ↑. 99% of my inspiration comes in the process. It's the place I strive to be

6. What's in your toolbox? Can you introduce us the tools and materials you use?
① Table vice   ③ Grinders (1250 x 3)
② Welding kit (TIG) ④ Lots and Lots of other stuff as well

7. Who in the field catches your attention most recently? Jon Pylypchuk (love this guy), Patricia Waller, Michael Rakowitz, Jan van Holleben, Fredeerdekens, Helmut Smits

8. Do you keep a collection of something as a hobby (not for work!)? What's the charm about?
oops → ⑨ I love dealing with social/political issues in my work, it allows me to feel superior to those that are being judged.

9. Your work seems to centre more around social scenes and humans recently when compared with the depiction of objects in the past. What do you want say to the world?
→ ⑧ I have a good portion of the covers of the New Yorker magazine from the last 10 years. I want to use it as wallpaper.

10. Please close your eyes and draft the first image in your mind.

#8 cont'd
◁ Just kidding, kinda. I was brought up very politically engaged and I think it's important that creative minds deal with these issues...

...and they are both very important for me

Gregory *Euclide*

1. How would you describe yourself?

I'm the type of person who would let other people do that.

2. What is your origin? What does your origin mean to you?

I look a lot like my father and grand. farmer and they were originally from French speaking Belgium. It really does not mean much to me because I believe we all come from roughly the same place if you go back far enough.

3. How do you describe what you're doing?

I'm thinking about my experience of land with a consideration of the landscape tradition. The process of making and displaying art as well as the use of land.

4. What do you find most playful and exciting in the creative process?

I enjoy seeing how ideas can become physical and how that process evolves over time.

5. Where do you get your inspirations? How do they inspire your creation?

I look at the world around me. I look to land and art – nature and institutions. The relationship between nature and art is very interesting and full of opportunity. These are loads of assumptions and contradictions to be found.

6. What's in your toolbox? Can you introduce us the tools and materials you use?

Most of the paintings are done in acrylic with water soluble pencils on paper. I like to use materials that can add to the meaning of the work like bubble wrap, PETG (the plastic used for packaging), wood, moss, model supplies... All have a meaningful presence in the work

7. Who in the field catches your attention most recently?

The center for land use interpretation is doing great work

8. Do you keep a collection of something as a hobby (not for work!)? What's the charm about?

I have a collection of lead and wood type as well as old cameras. I think I was interested in old forms of production that had a relationship to the body. Now every thing is so removed from the body and that will have some consequences in the future. How every one had to set type and develop prints by hand.

9. We find no humans in your work, or do we just fail to notice their appearance in the landscape?

We find evidence of their presence everywhere... farms, litter, buildings, names, art materials... But the actual people will not be found in the land

10. Please close your eyes and draft the first image in your mind.

Guerra *de la Paz*

THERE ARE 2 PEOPLE WHO MAKE UP GUERRA DE LA PAZ, ALAIN GUERRA & NERALDO DE LA PAZ

1. How would you describe yourself? *Guerra de la Paz is the composite name that represents the creative team efforts of Alain Guerra and Neraldo de la Paz. We live and work in Miami, Florida and have been consistently producing collaboratively since 1996.*

2. What is your origin? What does your origin mean to you? *We are Caribbean, Cuban born — Neraldo is from Matanzas, Alain from Havana, but our roots can be traced back to Celtic, Mediterranean and northern and west African influences. We find ourselves as global citizens & we connect to a diversity of customs within the European, African and Asian traditions. It is undeniable that our own DNA brings forth these tendencies that subliminally connects us to our ancestral roots.*

3. How do you describe what you're doing?

Making art. Creating visual conversation. It's what comes naturally — An organic process.

4. What do you find most playful and exciting in the creative process?
Working with found materials generates a sense of discovery. They possess a historic quality and a mysterious identity that invites curiosity.
Also, when there is spontaneity even though it's often followed by compulsion.

5. Where do you get your inspirations? How do they inspire your creation? *Inspiration can come from anywhere or anything. We are driven by information, so it can come from whatever we have been exposed to, actual or historic, natural or man-made. Our material is the force that drives our artistic existence — the meaning behind the work — the language that creates the image — the dialog that guides the process.*

6. What's in your toolbox? Can you introduce us the tools and materials you use?
Our hands and eyes are our most important tools. We have several toolboxes & they all serve a different purpose. Can we introduce our tools... it's vast — anything from a pencil to steel and concrete to a needle and thread or a found object. It depends on what it takes to realize our concepts.

7. Who in the field catches your attention most recently?

There are so many artists we admire (past and present) that it'd be difficult to single one out!

8. Do you keep a collection of something as a hobby (not for work!)? What's the charm about?
Because of our persistent collecting for work, we try to live minimally these days. One thing we have consistently amassed is music.
Music is motivating. We often listen to music while we work in our studio and it is nice to have a wide selection to choose from.

9. You have been sourcing discarded materials from the neighbourhood to compose art since 1996. How is it different from what you got now and in the past? How is it reflected in your work?
Today, many of the businesses that originally attracted us to the neighborhood have moved out and as the area becomes more gentrified, most of our sources get further away.
We live in a disposable culture in which the need to go "greener" is more evident than ever. People are more conscious about the mark their waste will leave on the environment & understand better what is needed to be done to reduce their footprint. Young people seem to be more aware of this. We're often led by the materials we acquire. For this, our work varies in technique and complexity. We can change direction simply by exploring the plasticity of the new material. This has allowed us to produce a multi-layered interdisciplinary body of work.

10. Please close your eyes and draft the first image in your mind.
Since we are two we would probably have different images. So we'll offer individual answers.

" I see darkness interrupted by little sparkles of light as if I am out in space looking into the infinite universe."

" Me too." :-)

Jeff *Nishinaka*

1. How would you describe yourself?

Low key, laid back, impatient, hyper, schizoid!

2. What is your origin? What does your origin mean to you?

Asian American. East meets west means the best of both worlds.

3. How do you describe what you're doing?

I make paperdolls... just kidding... well sometimes not!

4. What do you find most playful and exciting in the creative process?

Juggling ideas in the beginning... fast forward... seeing it all come together.

5. Where do you get your inspirations? How do they inspire your creation?

unexpected pleasant surprises, things that happen by chance. they inspire me to think outside the box.

6. What's in your toolbox? Can you introduce us the tools and materials you use?

tweezers, toothpicks, X-Acto knife, Elmers Glue-All. same basic tools since grade school... well, minus the X-Acto.

7. Who in the field catches your attention most recently?

Yuko Shimizu!

8. Do you keep a collection of something as a hobby (not for work!)? What's the charm about?

Everything Astro Boy. I've been a collector forever. my childhood hero!

9. You don't very much like to use colours in your work – unless otherwise required by clients, do you? What is it the thing you hope viewers could notice in your work?

I like using color, but only when necessary. I want viewers to see the sculptural quality of the paper.

10. Please close your eyes and draft the first image in your mind.

Zak ... world's greatest   dog!

Jennifer *Khoshbin*

1. How would you describe yourself?

A SERIES OF OPPOSITES!

WORKING NONSTOP <—> SLACKER AT HEART
WANT TO DO MORE FOR OTHERS <— OFTEN LAZY OR SELFISH
KNOW IT'S ABOUT THE PROCESS <— WOULD RATHER FINISH IT!

2. What is your origin? What does your origin mean to you?

I AM ITALIAN, JEWISH, IRISH WOMAN FROM PHILI. I AM RARELY ANY OF THESE THINGS, BUT OCCASIONALLY SOME, DEPENDING ON THE AFTERNOON.

3. How do you describe what you're doing? I DO WHAT MOST PEOPLE DO: FILL MY TIME WITH WHAT PLEASURE I CAN. FOR ME PERSONALLY, IT MEANS WORKING HARD AT MY ART, MY FAMILY, MY HOME, MY FRIENDSHIPS. MY ART SPECIFICALLY IS A STRADDLE BETWEEN DESIGN, CONTEMPORARY PHILOSOPHIES, FABLES, AND JUST-MAKE-SOMETHING.

4. What do you find most playful and exciting in the creative process?

COLLABORATING WITH OTHERS. DESIGNING OUR IDEAS, AND SLOWLY EXECUTING IT TOGETHER. POSSIBLY BECOMING SOMETHING DIFFERENT AFTER IT'S ALL OVER

5. Where do you get your inspirations? How do they inspire your creation?

I ATTEMPT TO BUILD ON MY WORK, CONSIDERING WHERE IT'S HEADED AND WHAT IT CAN UNCOVER EITHER MOMENTARILY, OR WITH LASTING EFFECTS. I LOOK TO OTHER CONTEMPORARY ARTISTS IN MY COMMUNITY AND BEYOND. IT'S A DIALOGUE

6. What's in your toolbox? Can you introduce us the tools and materials you use? BETWEEN US ALL.

MY TOOLBOX IS FILLED WITH: GLUE, CUTTING TOOLS, BOOKS, PAPER, PENCILS, ERASERS, BORROWED ILLUSTRATIONS, MATTE BOARDS, ANIMAL FORMS, RECORDING DEVICES, AND NOTES TO MYSELF.

7. Who in the field catches your attention most recently?

ANU TUOMINEN
LAUREN HAUPT
REBECCA WARD

8. Do you keep a collection of something as a hobby (not for work!)? What's the charm about?

I HAVE STOPPED KEEPING COLLECTIONS - ALTHOUGH HAVE HAD MANY IN THE PAST. NOW I TRY TO KEEP IT SIMPLE AND/OR USEFUL. A VINTAGE, WALL-MOUNTED PENCIL SHARPENER, A CROCHETED MOUSTACHE, A CERAMIC BIRD'S WING. NOT TOO MANY THINGS

9. Your work often depicts a swirl of words crafted out of some old fiction books. Were the JUST THE RIGHT contents of these books ever related to the work itself? What do words mean in your art? THINGS.

EACH ASPECT OF THE BOOK IS PART OF THE ENTIRE PIECE. WHAT THE TITLE INTIMATES OR THE STORY REFLECTS IS TIED TO BOTH THE ILLUSTRATION I CREATE AND THE WORD I ULTIMATELY PLACE IN THE CENTER OF THE CUTOUT. WORDS, STORIES, FABLES ARE WHAT CONNECTS MY BODY OF WORK. I LOVE LANGUAGE AND CANNOT SEEM TO GET AWAY FROM IT EVEN IF I SIMULTANEOUSLY BELIEVE THAT THIS WORLD IS UNDERSTOOD

10. Please close your eyes and draft the first image in your mind. THROUGH SOMETHING FAR BEYOND WORDS.
I AM A WORD GIRL.

Kenichi *Yokono*

1. How would you describe yourself??

I think of myself as an earnest person.
真面目だと思う。

2. What is your origin? What does your origin mean to you?

Picture books and Psychology. I think that the storyline is very important.
絵本と心理学。ストーリーが大切だと思う。

3. How do you describe what you're doing?

The starting point for me was to draw something I want have and I want to keep it for good. That principle hasn't changed from the beginning. Also, I came to realize that being an artist is the only way I can work in society. Simply, that's the reason for being an artist.

4. What do you find most playful and exciting in the creative process?

I mostly enjoy drawing rough sketches at the beginning of the process. I find joy when I feel the potential of creativity.
下書きを描いている時が一番楽しい。可能性に満ちている中に身を置いている時こそ喜びを感じます。

5. Where do you get your inspirations? How do you inspire your creation?

While watching movies, TV and driving a car, my ideas become clear.
 I don't listen to any music while creating my pieces.
映画やTVを見ながらやドライブ中に、アイデア、考えがまとまる。音楽は製作中にも聴きません。

6. What's in your toolbox? Can you introduce us the tools and materials you use?

3B pencil, tools for Suiboku-ga (ink-wash painting) and carving knives (a V-shaped gouge and U-shaped gouge).
3Bの鉛筆、水墨画用具、彫刻刀は角刀1本、丸刀1本のみ。

7. Who in the field has caught your attention the most recently?

I don't have any particular people I pay attention to as I am not an art fan or collector myself.
"注目"している人物はいない。アートファンやコレクターではないから。

8. Do you keep a collection of something as a hobby (not for work!)? What's the charm about?

Nothing.
ありません。

9. So, finally you have made a portrait of your family, with no ruins nor skulls but pure joy on the faces, and some self-portraits. Quite a change! How do you feel about the results?

Actually, I made this work on commission. For me, this work was like a celebratory piece for a newborn baby.
実はこの作品はコミッションワークで作ったものです。私にとっては子供が生まれた記念のようなもの。

10. Please close your eyes and draft the first image in your mind.

Mayuko *Fujino*

1. How would you describe yourself?

Paper Cutout Artist

2. What is your origin? What does your origin mean to you?

My origin is Japan. Though I don't live traditional style of life,
Japanese old culture developed my way of looking at spirituals and materials
on an unconscious level

3. How do you describe what you're doing?

The mixture of ① the papercut method influenced by Japanese traditional
and ② the collage in a contemporary style. designs

4. What do you find most playful and exciting in the creative process?

Each process gives me excitements so I can't choose one... ① When I am thinking of ideas,
I can live in the world of make-believe which I dreamed of in my childhood
Drafting is the process to make it become real, is simply fun, the pleasure of drawing lines comforts me

5. Where do you get your inspirations? How do they inspire your creation? ③ Cutting is a kind of
meditation

Music : is a guide for me to the outside world, encourages me by exposing
lives and feelings of other people

Books : They help me to decipher and understand the meanings of the images crawling in on my mind
Tokyo Bay Area : Too beautiful so I just can't help outputting the feeling it inputs me.

6. What's in your toolbox? Can you introduce us the tools and materials you use?

Pencils, ball-point pens, a cutter knife, sticky tapes, scissors,
a white sea shell (I use it as the container for replacement blades of my cutter knife

7. Who in the field catches your attention most recently?

Alda Carlson, who left a book of 1355 4leaf clovers that are pressed and glued in place
in decorative patterns. She was not actually an artist, I found her book on ebay, from the description:
"she never married and kept almost everything from her childhood" She started collecting 4leaf clover from
It's so BEAUTIFUL and I really want the book but unfortunately I couldn't afford it ... ☺ 1910.

8. Do you keep a collection of something as a hobby (not for work!)? What's the charm about?

I have small bells collection. I love them because of their each own sound / small music.
Their figures also fascinate me - first I only collected the bells designed in my favorite way, but now I'm trying to
buy every bells I find. By paying out of my own pocket for those bells I don't like so much, it almost became
like training for me to absorb the diversity of this world I live in and learn to accept the differences.

9. Tell us more about "Planet Platonic" – if Planet Platonic is your design practice, who is 'Arikui'?
What is 'Abduction' about?

"Planet Platonic" is the world I set for my previous story "Heavenly Bodies" and this "Arikui Abduction"
"Abduction" is the word about UFO/Aliens taking people away - I use it in that context.
"Arikui" means "Anteaters" in Japanese. They research the historical materials ✓

10. Please close your eyes and draft the first image in your mind.

"about "platonic", and now their purpose is to find "the Antman",
the mythical existence which is said to live underground of the planet.

one by one they abduct four-footed anteater (because anteaters
re brilliant with hunting ants), make it highly intellectual and biped walking
y the surgery implanting the pink foreign matter on its head.
ll those processes are for organizing the expedition to find the Antman.
n that way Arikuis are self-duplicating, but who did the first surgery
r the first Arikui?, It is still covered in mystery, the story is still going on
in my head.

Meredith *Dittmar*

1. How would you describe yourself?

Indescribable. The adjectives I'd pick change from moment
to moment.

2. What is your origin? What does your origin mean to you?

I'm a half Ukrainian, half Italian, American. My origin doesn't mean
much— I identify most with being human.

3. How do you describe what you're doing?

Describing what I do is always a chore. I usually say something along
the lines of "relief-like sculpture in polymer clay, mounted in shadowboxes."

4. What do you find most playful and exciting in the creative process?

Being in the flow -tapping into the silent space larger than self
that all creativity comes from.

5. Where do you get your inspirations? How do they inspire your creation?

I get inspiration from meditation and seeking the truth of things, and
from nature, mathematics, technology, and biology.

6. What's in your toolbox? Can you introduce us the tools and materials you use?

Polymer clay, liquid polymer, a pasta machine, tiles to sculpt on and move
parts around, a conventional oven, a pin, various blades and exacto knives,
sculpting tools, handmade tools, super glue, wire, plexiglass, stencils, spray paint

7. Who in the field catches your attention most recently?
+ more!

Marmots & mountain Goats.

8. Do you keep a collection of something as a hobby (not for work!)? What's the charm about?

I'm not a collector type really. I'd like to collect antiques but they
are out of my price range.

**9. You take commissions and do personal works such as clay illustrations and figure dolls at the
same time. How do you feel differently while you create?**

Creating fine art   is a lot deeper. For me it is about the truth of
existence and nothing else but what comes in the moment. Creating for a
client comes with constraints and an audience to please

10. Please close your eyes and draft the first image in your mind.

I cant draw nothingness! ◡

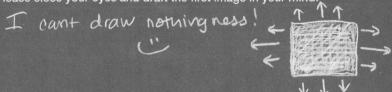

Michael *Velliquette*

1. How would you describe yourself?

A naturally curious person. Easily taken with things that sparkle & shine. I think best with my hands.

2. What is your origin? What does your origin mean to you?

I was raised to be joyful & hard working — and I think it informs much of what I do as an adult.

3. How do you describe what you're doing?

Pure magic

4. What do you find most playful and exciting in the creative process?

Getting the idea to make something, and then figuring out how to do it.

5. Where do you get your inspirations? How do they inspire your creation?

I'm very open to influence. I find myself most captivated with objects or events that are visually dense or optically complex.

6. What's in your toolbox? Can you introduce us the tools and materials you use?

It's all a very modest operation — paper, glue, scissors

7. Who in the field catches your attention most recently?

Brian Dettmer, Emma Van Leest, Oliver Herring, Mako Ueda....

8. Do you keep a collection of something as a hobby (not for work!)? What's the charm about?

I have an eclectic collection of small found objects (2"x2" ea.) I keep them on a big shelf in a hallway — it is silly & quirky but also pleasing to look at.

9. You've run an art space with Leslee Fraser and Joey Fauerso but decided to take a hiatus after three years of operation in 2005. How was that decision made? What happened afterwards?

We all had opportunities to pursue w/ our own work, which we are still doing.

10. Please close your eyes and draft the first image in your mind.

Nina *Braun*

1. How would you describe yourself?

A peruvian giant otter.

2. What is your origin? What does your origin mean to you?

DIY

3. How do you describe what you're doing?

I blend the traditional with the contemporary.

4. What do you find most playful and exciting in the creative process?

Right now I enjoy the analogue creation of unique pieces.

5. Where do you get your inspirations? How do they inspire your creation?

I get inspiration by using a mind-expanding technique: the knitting-meditation!

6. What's in your toolbox? Can you introduce us the tools and materials you use?

All kinds of needles, threads, fabrics, wadding and doll-eyes.

7. Who in the field catches your attention most recently?

Mickry 3.net and Michael Swaney.com

8. Do you keep a collection of something as a hobby (not for work!)? What's the charm about?

Not really. Being able to let go means having both hands free. (I learned that during the knitting-meditation!)

9. You have made a few stop-motion pictures and cartoons too – 'Business Today' and 'Going Around the House'. How did you find the results? Can you tell us more about the two?

A client / collector gave me the chance to explore 2 new techniques: stop-trick & whiteboard animation. I liked the associative work without storyboard.

10. Please close your eyes and draft the first image in your mind.

Roman *Klonek*

1. How would you describe yourself?

I'm a quite tall man (2 meter), living in quite small town (Düsseldorf) and be a member of a very nice artist collective called „Dadaluxe". Our studio is 2 km from my flat and I love to walk this way every day...

2. What is your origin? What does your origin mean to you?

I was born in Kattowice/Poland. My family moved to Germany when I was 3 years old. There are no memories — merely subconsciously but clearly I feel an affection for Poland. I'm there almost every summer for hiking tours... there is a warm connection.

3. How do you describe what you're doing?

I do commissioned illustrations and in between woodcut printings. I have a diary/sketchbook and try to illustrate every day but 90% of this is crap but that's ok as long as I got my 10%

4. What do you find most playful and exciting in the creative process?

To catch an idea suddenly. And then to realize that this one is really good. Even after 3 times thinking over it.

5. Where do you get your inspirations? How do they inspire your creation?

I don't have any inspiration strategy but one thing is for sure: A relaxed situation is the best condition for a good mind flow. Actually I draw a lot while reading ... OK concrete: Old Russian literature is very inspiring.

6. What's in your toolbox? Can you introduce us the tools and materials you use?

For woodcut printing: Knifes, chisels, wood (cottonwood, poplar), very viscous colors, rollers, thick paper

7. Who in the field catches your attention most recently?

Takashi Murakami, David O'Reilly, Victor Castillo, Marco Wagner, AJ Fosik

8. Do you keep a collection of something as a hobby (not for work!)? What's the charm about?

Sorry no collections, well ...ok music.

9. You believe that people's mind follows their language and vice versa. How is it so? Which culture/language interests you most?

Every culture got their focal points and on the other hand, less important issues. Its hard for me to imagine that, for example, natives from the Amazonas don't got numbers. They're counting 1, 2 ...a lot. They don't even got a word for „numeracy". Nevertheless they organize their life. Well another kind of logic ... But, well, I mostly interested in Polish and Russian culture. This must sound strange but they have especially the Russians and especially in their language a kind of roughness and rudeness that is impolite & attractive in the same time. Even the appearance of the type ist very expressive.

10. Please close your eyes and draft the first image in your mind.

Ron *van der Ende*

1. How would you describe yourself?

Sculptor / Craftsman. Work aholic. Father. Music Lover.

2. What is your origin? What does your origin mean to you?

I practically grew up in a carpenteres work shop. I chose the
Art Academy to become a painter. You could say I came full circle!

3. How do you describe what you're doing?

I do -perspectively correct- BAS RELIEF/MOSAICS in SZAVENGed
Timbers.

4. What do you find most playful and exciting in the creative process?

Having a piece come together 'on the fly'. Having my hands
think for me.

5. Where do you get your inspirations? How do they inspire your creation?

I browse books and web image Archives for input. Choices are made
by Assessing visual impact, thematical and sculptural strength and
technical challenge

6. What's in your toolbox? Can you introduce us the tools and materials you use?

As materials old wood, doors mostly. As tools an Overhead projector.
a Sawing table to rip apart the doors, A planer And belt sander. A knife.
A hammer. Tens of thousands of nails

7. Who in the field catches your attention most recently?

.. Eric Yahuker. Amazing drawings! clever, silly and Tenacious!

8. Do you keep a collection of something as a hobby (not for work!)? What's the charm about?

Vintage company technical handbooks and promotional stuff
like jig-saw puzzles etc. For love of their detail and style

9. Sometimes you accompany your work with relevant images at the back. Do you expect the audience to notice their presence? Why do you incorporate these pictures in your work?

The Audience is usually UNAWARE of the background images. They Are
there for the enjoyment of the people that get to handle my stuff.

10. Please close your eyes and draft the first image in your mind.

Sarah *Trahan*

1. How would you describe yourself?

A CONFIDENT CONTRADICTION, IN ALL WAYS.

2. What is your origin? What does your origin mean to you?

I GREW UP WITH CRAYONS AND BOOKS AND A VERY ACTIVE IMAGINATION. MY PARENTS ALWAYS ENCORAGED THIS AND MADE SURE I HAD OUTLETS TO EXPRESS MYSELF CREATIVELY. I DON'T THINK I WOULD BE ABLE TO DO WHAT I DO NOW WITHOUT THAT KIND OF UPBRINGING.

3. How do you describe what you're doing?

TAKING THINGS THAT INTEREST ME AND WEAVING THEM IN TO ODD, OPEN-ENDED LITTLE NARRATIVES.... RE-INTERPRETING SCALE AND SURFACE, USING MY VERY OVERACTIVE IMAGINATION.

4. What do you find most playful and exciting in the creative process?

STUMBLING ACROSS THE PERFECT TEXTURE IN A FLEA MARKET, AND ALL OF THE HAPPY ACCIDENTS THAT HAPPEN WHEN I START TO COLLAGE THINGS TOGETHER ON THE COMPUTER - AND OF COURSE, THE FINISHED PRODUCT (I LOVE IT WHEN A PLAN COMES TOGETHER ☺)

5. Where do you get your inspirations? How do they inspire your creation?

I AM AN OBSERVER, SO I AM INSPIRED BY ALL THINGS VISUAL. I LOVE SMALL DETAILS - LIKE A TINY LEAF OR RUFFLES. ON A DRESS. I'M CONSTANTLY THINKING - HOW CAN I USE THAT IN A DIFFERENT WAY?

6. What's in your toolbox? Can you introduce us the tools and materials you use?

MY TOOLBOX CONSISTS OF PILES OF VINTAGE KNICKNACKS AND FABRIC REMNANTS, COLORED PENCILS, PENS, GRAPHITE, ACRYLIC PAINT, OLD PHOTOS, A FLATBED SCANNER AND MY MACBOOK PRO,...

7. Who in the field catches your attention most recently?

REED + RADER, THEIR FASHION WORK COMBINING STILL AND MOVING IMAGES IS REALLY FANTASTIC AND SOMETIMES CREEPY WHICH I REALLY LIKE.

8. Do you keep a collection of something as a hobby (not for work!)? What's the charm about?

I COLLECT VINTAGE CLOTHING FROM THE 1930'S AND 40'S - THERE'S SOMETHING ABOUT THE STYLE AND GLAMOUR OF THAT ERA THAT I REALLY LOVE.

9. You have told us it was the character and stories of the old things that interest you most, but your work reflects your fascination about the future too. What is your future like?

MORE MAKING AND COLLECTING! HOPEFULLY MY FUTURE IS FULL OF MORE OLD STUFF AND MORE NEW TECHNOLOGY - AND MORE SPACE TO PUT IT IN.

10. Please close your eyes and draft the first image in your mind.

Severija *Inčirauskaitė-Kriaunevičiene*

1. How would you describe yourself? My name is Severija Inčirauskait Kriauneviciene
I am an artist, curator and teacher.

2. What is your origin? What does your origin mean to you?
I was born in Lithuania. So, I am Lithuanian. It means my language, nature,
traditions, "life style" to me.

3. How do you describe what you're doing?
I creak art objects, installations about our lives realities

4. What do you find most playful and exciting in the creative process?
The most exciting and important thing in the art creation is the beginning-
generating of idea. Context, situations and reason of the emergence of art
work.

5. Where do you get your inspirations? How do they inspire your creation?
Daily life moments, things from our surrounding, pop culture, kitsch
inspires me and my art.

6. What's in your toolbox? Can you introduce us the tools and materials you use?
My tools are: paper, pencil, computer, Drill, drill bits, a lot of
colored yarn, and different old things from our daily life

7. Who in the field catches your attention most recently?

Generally I use the old utilitarian objects and transform them into
works of art. But currently I'm trying to keep the utilitarian aspect.
I try to creak objects that can be works of art as well as design
objects. For example my collection "Way of roses" (tuning of car and
installation at the same time) or collection "A bucket of light" (floor
lamps and sculptures at the same time.

8. Do you keep a collection of something as a hobby (not for work!)? What's the charm about?

I can't stop collecting old (not antique) things from villages
which I plan to use for art creation. But very often they
remain unused. So, I have a big collection of this kind of
old things. Especially I like the old rusted objects.

9. When did you first discover pleasure in things that others consider insignificant? What have you found in them?

I don't remember exactly but I think "Always in fashion"
was the first of my recycled works. In this work I transformed
old Slavic style wraps (which are popular among old women)
into sport caps (for young people).
Old object has it's own history, energy, associations.
When you use them purposefull for expressing your ideas,
you can tell a lot. Because old things are very eloquent.
I like it.

10. Please close your eyes and draft the first image in your mind.

Studio *Evelin Kasikov*

1. How would you describe yourself?

Serious. Very.

2. What is your origin? What does your origin mean to you?

I am from Estonia which is a small country with just over 1.3 m people. My background is important for me, I think my work is influenced by Estonian language, culture and craft traditions.

3. How do you describe what you're doing?

I am a creator, a visual communicator. My work can take many forms but is always connected to typography in some way

4. What do you find most playful and exciting in the creative process?

looking behind the obvious, discovering something you never expected to find.

5. Where do you get your inspirations? How do they inspire your creation?

From my surroundings, from books, from other people London is such a creative hub, there is always something going on.

6. What's in your toolbox? Can you introduce us the tools and materials you use?

My mind, my eyes, my hands, my MacBook.
They are not that different.

7. Who in the field catches your attention most recently?

I love the work of Anthony Burrill. Very bold and minimal, yet warm and human. Most recently seen on the cover of Creative Review

8. Do you keep a collection of something as a hobby (not for work!)? What's the charm about?

I do have a collection old theatre programmes, it is not very organized but I keep them as memories of great experiences.

9. You have been looking into the ways people perceive visual messages through a variety of mixed tech and media. What are the interesting things we might have neglected while we see?

My work plays with the illusion of seeing. I often use different viewpoints and distances in the same image - this is a different seeing experience.

10. Please close your eyes and draft the first image in your mind.

I am in Tallinn when writing this. My house is by the sea, when I close my eyes I see my favourite image.

Walton *Creel*

1. How would you describe yourself?

I enjoy driving around aimlessly in my car.

2. What is your origin? What does your origin mean to you?

I grew up in Alabama, which is in the southeastern United States. If I lived in a place more commonly associated with art, not only would I not have been inspired to work with guns, but I would not have the access to a place to actually shoot my art in peace.

3. How do you describe what you're doing?

I use thousands of bullet holes to create large format images.

4. What do you find most playful and exciting in the creative process?

Designing the pattern is the most open-ended part of what I do. I enjoy the subtleties that a dot here and there can have on an entire image.

5. Where do you get your inspirations? How do they inspire your creation?

Usually when I am not expecting it. One idea can lead to an entire group of works.

6. What's in your toolbox? Can you introduce us the tools and materials you use?

1 .22 caliber Ruger 10/22, thousands of bullets, 5 clips, 1 gun cleaning kit, 1 box for catching used bullet casings, transfer pattern, 72x48 inch white painted and reinforced sheet of aluminum, lots of tape, 1 pickup truck.

7. Who in the field catches your attention most recently?

I love Chris Burden, especially his more recent works like the Two Minute Airplane Factory, which consisted of a completely automated machine that built and launched balsa wood airplanes every two minutes.

8. Do you keep a collection of something as a hobby (not for work!)? What's the charm about?

Deer antlers. My girlfriend and I have a goal of collecting enough to cover a wall. Hopefully the cats won't hurt themselves.

9. Your calibre rifle is a present from your father. For sure making illustrations with it wasn't his intention! Did he ever say anything about how you use your gun?

Dad is my biggest supporter. He loves what I am doing with the gun he gave me. He has a barbershop and tells all his customers about me.

10. Please close your eyes and draft the first image in your mind.

Yulia *Brodskaya*

1. How would you describe yourself?

intuitivexcellentalantedirecthoughtfuluckyulia

2. What is your origin? What does your origin mean to you?

I was born in Moscow (Russia), my origin means that Russian is my native language

3. How do you describe what you're doing?

'papergkaphic' illustrations

4. What do you find most playful and exciting in the creative process?

Listening to audiobooks while doing 'the paper work'

5. Where do you get your inspirations? How do they inspire your creation?

designers blogs, image bookmarking websites - I enjoy diversity

6. What's in your toolbox? Can you introduce us the tools and materials you use?

Endless piles of paper & card, scissors, glue, cocktail straws & sticks
— for rolling

7. Who in the field catches your attention most recently?

Kiei Takano

8. Do you keep a collection of something as a hobby (not for work!)? What's the charm about?

hope, I only collect paper & card (for work!)

9. It's been five to six years since you have moved to the UK. How do you find life there? If you ever want a change, which would be the next possible city you would like to experience life?

Toronto maybe, but at the moment I'm absolutely fine here

10. Please close your eyes and draft the first image in your mind.

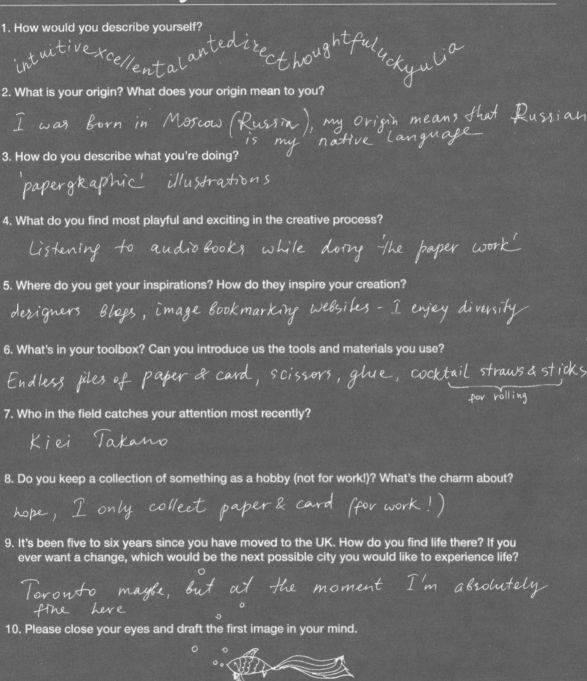

Illustration • *Play* 2

An Expedition to the Extraordinary

First published and distributed by
viction:workshop ltd.

viction:ary™

Unit C, 7th Floor, Seabright Plaza,
9-23 Shell Street, North Point, Hong Kong
URL: www.victionary.com
Email: we@victionary.com

Edited and produced by viction:workshop ltd.

Book design by viction:workshop ltd.
Concepts & art direction by Victor Cheung

ISBN 978-988-17328-6-6

Printed and bound in China

Acknowledgements

The successful completion of this book rests on a number of
parties. In no specific order, we would like to thank all the
designers, companies and producers who have contributed to the
compilation of this book. Our success also owes a great deal to
the many professionals who have given us precious insights and
comments throughout the entire process. And, to the many whose
names are not published here, we thank you for your specific input
and continuous support the whole time. The book would not have
been accomplished without your significant help.

Future Editions

If you wish to contribute to the next edition of
Victionary publications, please email us your details
to submit@victionary.com.